D-Day and Beyond

A True Story of Escape and POW Survival

Julie M. Phend
Stanley E. Edwards, Jr.

For David,
"Make every day
count!"
Julie M. Phend

BURD STREET PRESS
SHIPPENSBURG, PENNSYLVANIA

This Burd Street Press publication
was printed by
Beidel Printing House, Inc.
63 West Burd Street
Shippensburg, PA 17257-0708 USA

The acid-free paper used in this book meets the guidelines for permanence and durability of the Committee on Production Guidelines for Book Longevity of the Council on Library Resources.

For a complete list of available publications
please write
Burd Street Press
Division of White Mane Publishing Company, Inc.
P.O. Box 708
Shippensburg, PA 17257-0708 USA

Library of Congress Cataloging-in-Publication Data

Phend, Julie M., 1948-
    D-Day and beyond : a true story of escape and POW survival / Julie M. Phend, Stanley E. Edwards, Jr.
        p. cm.
    Includes bibliographical references and index.
    ISBN 1-57249-362-3 (alk. paper)
    1. Edwards, Stanley E., 1923- 2. World War, 1939-1945--Prisoners and prisons, German. 3. World War, 1939-1945--Personal narratives, American. 4. Prisoners of war--United States--Biography. 5. Prisoners of war--Germany--Biography. 6. Survival after airplane accidents, shipwrecks, etc. 7. Prisoner of war escapes--Germany. 8. World War, 1939-1945--Aerial operations. American. I. Edwards, Stanley E., 1923- II. Title.

D805.G3P463 2004
940.54'72'092--dc22
[B]
                                                                        2004048715

Contents

Illustrations & Maps

Author's Note

I first met Stan Edwards when he came to the school where I am a teacher to talk to our students about World War II. I was captivated by his story of a young pilot shot down on D-Day and forced to survive in a foreign country while a war was going on. Afterward, I spoke to him about preserving his story—I was thinking of video or audiotape, but he said, "Yes, I've been looking for someone to write the book." Without even thinking, I volunteered for the job. And that's how our partnership began.

Separated from his military unit in a foreign country, Stanley Edwards was cut off from news sources, ignorant of military plans, and unable to speak the language. He had to swallow his fear, gather his courage, and do whatever it took to survive. After the war, he was left to piece his experiences into the larger puzzle that was World War II. In some ways, he spent his lifetime doing that.

This is a true story. But it is a story colored by memory—and memory has a way of distorting events; one image stands out with crystal clarity, another is shrouded in fog. Memories are colored by emotion, softened by time, and shaped by what we learn later, so that sometimes we're left saying, "That *must* have been how it was."

Like many veterans, Stan did not talk about his experiences immediately after the war. He and his young wife, Shirley, were anxious to put the trauma of those years behind them and begin a new life. But ten years later, when Stan was working for International Harvester, the company magazine decided to do a story on their veterans and taped an interview with Stan. That was the beginning. Later he joined the Association of Former Prisoners of Stalag Luft III, where he was able to connect with other prisoners and collectively begin to make sense of their experiences. He began to talk to his own children, telling them stories around the dinner table. And when his daughter Liz became a history teacher, she asked her father to come in and talk to her students. To help himself remember, Stan taped the story of his experiences.

All of this previous talk made my job easier. Still, piecing together the chronology and geography was a challenge. I would listen to a section of the tape, interview him at length to get details, research to corroborate the facts and fill in the holes, and then write the incident. Sometimes I would get it just right the first time, and he would beam, "Yes, that's exactly how it was." Other times, he would clarify, "No, it wasn't like that—it was like . . ." In this way, we worked until we had a complete draft, and I gave it to him to read. But it wasn't right yet.

I will never forget how he came back to me after reading that finished draft and confessed, "There are some things I haven't told you." Those were the stories he *wasn't* proud of, the stories he hadn't ever talked about, the ones he'd edited from his oral history. But they were engraved in his memory, and he knew they needed to be included if this book was to be true. And by that time, telling the true story had become a passion. In the process of talking and writing, Stan was able to make sense of the events of his life and to appreciate what is important. You have only to read the chapter on Reflections to know that.

Stan Edwards died on April 4, 2004, just months before this book was published. I'm so sorry that he didn't live to see it in print, but very glad we completed it. I feel privileged to have been part of Stanley Edwards's life and witness to his story.

—Julie Phend

Preface

World War II Begins

After World War I, several countries in Europe were disappointed and bitter, leaving them vulnerable to dictators who promised them a better life. One of these countries was Germany, ruled by Adolf Hitler, who told people that their troubles were all because of the Jews. He vowed to get rid of the Jews and promised that Germany would again be great if the people followed him.

World War II officially began on September 1, 1939, when Hitler's German army invaded Poland. Two days later, Britain and France declared war on Germany. At first, the United States under President Franklin Roosevelt vowed to stay neutral, but after France surrendered in 1940 and Britain was left fighting alone, the U.S. agreed to supply Britain with arms and ships. By June of 1941, Roosevelt agreed that defeating Hitler outweighed everything else.

Then, on December 7, 1941, the Japanese (Hitler's allies) launched a surprise attack on the United States at Pearl Harbor, Hawaii, and Congress declared war on Japan. Two days later, Germany and Italy declared war on the United States.

The attack on Pearl Harbor brought the United States firmly together in support of the war. Six million men and women enlisted in the armed forces, 10 million more were drafted, war plants worked overtime to supply arms to the Allied Forces, and civilians planted victory gardens and worked for the Red Cross making up supply packages to send overseas. Everybody became involved.

Acknowledgments

Most of all, I'm grateful to Stanley Edwards, for sharing his life with me and giving me the opportunity to write his extraordinary story. I'm also grateful to Stephen Ambrose, who wrote the wonderful book *D-Day*, which gave me a much deeper understanding of the big picture, to the veterans of The Association of Former Prisoners of Stalag Luft III, whose efforts at preserving their stories and photographs have been most helpful; to the United States Air Force Academy for allowing the use of the pictures on their website (see below); to Stan's family, especially his daughters Elizabeth Wick and Margaret Wolfe, for their enthusiasm and support of this project, and to WGN reporter Chuck Coppola, for his interest and promotion of our efforts.

I'm deeply grateful to my colleagues, friends, and family for reading drafts, listening to my concerns, and offering advice and support: especially to my sister Jan Oldenburg; my husband, Jack Phend; and my children, Jennifer and Nicholas Phend. To friends Susan Greenwood, Jean Guenther, Alice Guzman, Tom McKay, Mary McVicker, Janet Reed, Diane Walter, Bonita Slovinski, and Amy Vose. I couldn't have done it without you.

Finally I'm grateful to the staff at White Mane Publishing, especially Harold Collier, Nicole Riley, and Marianne Zinn, for their interest in the book and for their patience in answering all my many questions.

Photographs are provided courtesy of Clark Special Collections Branch, United States Air Force Academy, McDermott Library, and The Friends of the Air Force Academy Library. The materials on the Academy Library's Stalag Luft III web pages reside at the USAFA Library, and were donated to our library by Albert P. Clark, Lt. Gen., USAFA, Ret., various other "Kriegies" and others.

—Julie Phend

Map of Flight from
U.S. to England

900 Miles

Map by Elizabeth Wick

Fort Wayne,
Indiana

West Palm Beach,
Florida

Puerto Rico

Georgetown,
British Guyana

Belém,
Brazil

Natal,
Brazil

Ascension
Island

Roberts Field,
Liberia

Dakar,
French West Africa

Marrakech,
Morocco

Exeter Airfield,
Great Britain

Chapter One

Before the Invasion

Stanley Edwards as
air force cadet, 1943

Author collection

As I climbed into the C-47 and adjusted the controls, I felt the excitement and nervous tension in the pit of my stomach. D-Day had finally arrived. The long-promised invasion was about to begin. I was 21 years old, and a first lieutenant with the army's 82nd Airborne Division. My job as copilot was to fly into Normandy with a crew of five to drop 18 paratroopers into the combat zone. We were all geared up, anxious to get on with the job. In spite of the tension in the air, the paratroopers were in pretty good spirits, eager to get in, get it over with, and have it done.

In the silence before takeoff, I reflected on the steps that had brought me here. Flying planes had always come naturally to me. I'd grown up around airfields and worked for United Airlines as a kid. One time, I drove a person who owned an airfield to the hospital. His wife was having a baby and there was half a foot of snow on the ground. As we drove, we talked, and he learned of my interest in flying. Afterward, he arranged lessons for me, and I earned a limited commercial license. I enlisted in the army on April 8, 1941, when I was 18 years old and worked my way up through the ranks of private, private first class, corporal, and sergeant as a weather forecaster. I liked predicting the weather and was good at it, but I still had a yearning to fly. So, even though my commanding officer recommended me for West Point Officers' Training School, I chose flying school.

Stan, *left*, with flight school buddies, 1943

Author collection

Flying school was easy for me. I often had free time because I'd tested out of some of the courses, and I spent much of that time hanging around the hangars making friends with the mechanics and learning about the planes. I was first in my class to solo, and in December of 1943, I graduated. There were 88 graduates in my class out of the 210 who'd begun the course. There was a war going on in Europe, of course, and pilots were needed over there. So immediately after graduation, I went to Austin, Texas, to C-47 transition school and then to Granada, Mississippi, to tactical school. In order to go overseas as a first pilot, a soldier had to first fly two hundred hours in the aircraft. My crew and I had 27 days to do it before we were scheduled to leave. Most days, that meant 12 hours of straight flying time. But with delays for weather, there were days when we flew from 6:00 A.M. until midnight and went to bed at 2:00 A.M., just to get up the next morning and do it all again. But this was all part of the process of getting ready to fly overseas.

Normally, the same crew flew together week after week until they knew each other so well they were a well-oiled team. Nothing any crewmember did would be a surprise; the utter predictability of it would ensure a safe and orderly flight. But a recent tragedy meant that I was flying with an entirely new crew. The weekend I finished my training, I went to Chicago to visit my sweetheart, Shirley Broecker, the girl who would later become my wife. While I was gone, another pilot borrowed my crew so he could log more hours. He flew the plane in a storm; it crashed, and everyone in the crew was killed. When I came back from Chicago and learned that everyone was dead, I was stunned. I couldn't believe it! They gave me the option of some time off, but I decided instead to continue with the plan to go overseas. I was anxious to be of service.

I was put into a new crew as copilot, and we were off. Now, flying overseas in a C-47 isn't a straight shot. Because a C-47 is a relatively small plane, it can't fly directly overseas.

C-47

The C-47 was the military version of the DC-3, a twin-engine plane built by Douglas Aircraft in the 1930s. Also known as the Dakota, the C-47 was unarmed and unarmored, designed to carry a stick (one planeload) of 18 paratroopers. The plane was slow—its top speed was 230 miles per hour—but it was rugged and well designed, well suited to its D-Day mission.

C-47 in flight

Author collection, Grenada Army
Air Field yearbook, 1943

Instead, there are a series of stops that allow you to perform
necessary checks and refuel before going on. We picked up our
C-47 in Ft. Wayne, Indiana, on March 9, 1944. Our first stop
was to be West Palm Beach, Florida, where we would receive
our orders. Even then, it wasn't an auspicious beginning. There
was a blinding snowstorm that morning in Ft. Wayne, but
planes were still flying out. We had just set the gyrocompass
when the engine went out. Not knowing whether the engine
was going to conk out or if it was just the gage malfunction-
ing, we decided to go back. We flew in a tight circle about 150
feet in the air, looking for the field. In the snowstorm, it wasn't
easy to find. Finally, we spotted the field; we dropped full flaps,
cutting the throttle back, and hit about midway down the runway. It turned out to be the wrong runway, but at least we
were on the ground. We went in for a check, learned it was
just instrument failure and easily fixed, and we set off again
the next morning, once again in a snowstorm. This time we
made it to Morrison Field in West Palm Beach.

There we picked up our orders. We weren't allowed to
open them until we were three miles outside the limits of the
United States. All we knew until we were in the air was that
our next stop was Borinquen Field in Puerto Rico. Once we
were outside the United States, we opened the orders and
learned that we were headed to England.

On the way to Borinquen Field, our automatic pilot went
out, and we had to fly the plane manually. At Borinquen, we
tried to get it fixed, but we couldn't. So rather than wait, we set
off, wanting to stay with the group we had been with through
training. From Puerto Rico, we flew to Georgetown, British
Guyana. The trees on either side of the runway were at least
one hundred feet high. It was like landing in a funnel. After we
landed, we ate in the officer's mess, but we'd barely started
when we were told to hurry up and finish because a special
guest was coming. Lo and behold, it was Mrs. Roosevelt, the
president's wife! We all lined up outside to watch her arrival.

Security around her was very tight; in fact, two planes that looked exactly the same landed on the field at the exact time so no one could be sure which plane she was in. She got off the plane accompanied by several Secret Service men, looking exactly like she did in the newspaper pictures. She waved to all of us and said a few words about what a great thing we were doing for our country. It was all very exciting. I later learned that she was visiting all the bases in the Caribbean to inspect them and give moral support to the troops.

After Georgetown we flew to Belém, Brazil, at the mouth of the Amazon River. There, it rained every afternoon about 3:00, and 20-foot-deep ditches surrounded the field to collect the water. It was pouring when we got there and we had to circle the field until the rain stopped. When we finally landed, I went off to file a flight plan. While I was gone, the pilot decided to move the plane and taxied on the slippery runway straight into one of those deep ditches. One of the wing tips on the plane broke, so we ended up staying there for three days. We had to disassemble the right wheel because sand and mud had damaged the landing gear. We cleaned it all up and reassembled it. Luckily, I knew how to do that, having spent all those hours working in the hangars during flying school!

Finally, we were off, flying south and east from Belém to Natal on the east coast of Brazil, then to Ascension Island. The flight from Natal to Ascension was 10 hours long, all over water—no landmarks to guide us. I asked the navigator if he knew how to "shoot the moon," using the moon and stars to find out our location. He hadn't had much experience using a sextant, so we reviewed it together. Twice during the flight we had to change our compass headings. But at 8:45 A.M. we contacted the airfield and were told we had clearance to land in 10 minutes. It was an awful runway, uphill at first, then sharply down. But somehow we managed it safely.

From there we flew up to Roberts Field in Liberia. At each field we were given the colors of the day. The rule was that if we flew over any task forces or ships, we had to fire a volley pistol to identify the plane as American. The flares were a different color each day, and that day they were green. But going from Ascension to Roberts Field, nobody in the crew could find the green flares to put into the volley pistol. As we neared the ships, we became really worried. What if we couldn't fire the flare and were mistaken for an enemy plane? Eventually, however, the flares were found; we fired one, and landed safely at Roberts Field.

We spent one day there, then flew up to Dakar in French West Africa. We spent a day at that field, and the next morning prepared to head out. We were the third plane in line waiting to take off. Ahead of us a B-24 waited, then a B-17, then our C-47. The B-24 took off and everything seemed normal. Then the B-17 took off. It got about 50 feet in the air, then nosed into the ground at the end of the runway. We watched in horror as the plane blew up and started on fire. We had our radio on with the tower, of course, and just then they got a call. The B-24 had also crashed—on the beach about five miles from the field. So they closed the airfield and didn't let any other planes take off that day. We never learned why they crashed; it was probably just coincidence, but it was incidents like this that made me realize how close the line was between life and death, and I wasn't even in the war yet!

We took off from Dakar the next day without incident and went up to Marrakech in Morocco on the northeastern coast of Africa. On the way, we ran into a dust storm up at about 13,000 feet. We fought our way through those mountains battling the dust, then rain, eventually flying through a narrow pass. Bigger airplanes could just climb over the mountains at about 17,000 feet, but we had a full load of fuel going over and we couldn't climb that high. Finally, we got through the pass and landed at Marrakech, spending a day there. Our goal was finally in sight—one more flight and we'd be in England.

We took off from Marrakech at 11:30 at night and flew out over the Atlantic. We'd been told that we'd pass a lighthouse on the southwest tip of Portugal. Suddenly, lights were going by us on the left side instead of on the right where we expected them. I called out to the navigator, "Check on this. I don't think we're where we oughta be." Sure enough, the winds had blown us off-course, and we were inland over Spain headed straight west, not at the tip of Portugal at all. So we headed out to sea, picked up the right course and flew to England, about a nine and one-half-hour flight. When we landed at Exeter airfield, we were given our final orders. We were to report to the airfield at Grantham, England, two hundred miles due north of London. It was March 28, 1944. It had taken us 19 days to get to England.

Ever since then, I'd been stationed at Grantham, practicing dropping gliders and paratroopers, writing letters, and finding ways to pass the time with the other soldiers. We knew that a major Allied offensive was being planned and that we were to be part of it, but we didn't know when it would come. In the meantime, a little gambling added some spice to an otherwise dull life of waiting for action. All the guys on base played cards—blackjack and poker being the favorites. The problem was, none of us had much money to gamble with, so we came up with some schemes. For instance, our airfield gave us punch cards for dinners. At the end of the month, they paid a quarter for every meal not punched. Somebody got the idea that we could eat dinners on other bases and collect the money. So we'd often fly off to another base for dinner—the other bases never punched the card, and at the end of the month we'd cash in and pocket the change, which went into the gambling fund. We'd even gamble on the job. Sometimes before flying practice, we'd each contribute a quarter to the pot. Then the crew chiefs would warm up the planes and we'd race to take off. Whoever got off the ground first would win the pot. When our squadron commander found out, we really caught it, but it was fun while it lasted.

Sometimes I'd be called on to fly to another field in southern England or the northern coast of Ireland to pick up wounded soldiers who were being sent back to the U.S. There was always a nurse assigned to the flight to tend to the wounded. One of my favorites was a big, fun-loving woman named Maggie who smoked cigars. "Hey, Stan," she'd say, "have you got a cigar? How about letting me fly the plane?" So one day coming back from Neets Corner I let her fly for a while. "You want to try landing it?" I asked when we got near the field. "Naw," she replied, "I'm not ready for that." Thank goodness she chickened out because unbeknownst to me, we had blown a tire on take-off, and that was one of the roughest landings I'd ever had to make!

I also spent a lot of time writing letters to Shirley. I missed her terribly and wanted to tell her every detail of how I spent my time. In my letters, I romantically professed my undying love for her and dreamed of our future together once the war ended. But, like the other soldiers on base, I wanted to see some action. I was tired of just sitting around waiting for something to happen.

Then in mid-April, one of the officers came in and asked if anyone would like to volunteer for special mission training. This was training for a C-47 outfit that would be working one hundred feet off the ground to drop equipment and paratroopers to the underground in France. Jumping at the chance to do something at last, I volunteered for the training, along with another young man in the squadron. When we got there, though, the training was much different than I had expected. We were trained to use weapons and to kill people with our bare hands and feet. They gave us a lot of equipment, including two knives, a two-inch and a six-inch, two firearms, one that was tiny and strapped onto the ankle, and a small pillbox containing two cyanide pills. We learned that we should take cyanide rather than give away any government secrets if we were being tortured. As a result of this training, I knew more about weapons and killing than the average C-47 pilot, but I didn't feel very comfortable with it. I doubted whether I would ever be able to kill someone, and I certainly didn't intend to use the cyanide!

The training lasted about three weeks. When we returned to the base in May, I tried to tell the other guys about it. They didn't believe me—they said I was just bragging. So I stopped talking about it, and even tried to stop thinking about it.

One night I was called on to fly up to Glasgow to pick up a three-star general and his aides and fly them to a big invasion planning meeting in London. By this time, that was all we heard about—D-Day, planned for some time at the beginning of June. Now our activity sped up. In mid-May, we flew a dummy mission over England, using the same headings and dropping paratroopers exactly as we would in the invasion. On June 2, everyone was restricted to the base. No more flying out for dinner—no more flying anywhere. We were told that the invasion was to take place on June 5. Our big mission had come at last! Still, we played cards and concentrated on the winnings as if that were the most important thing going on in the world. I played blackjack, and at one point, I was ahead by 1,000 pounds (about $5,000)—then I got the deal and lost it all.

On June 4, we had a big briefing from 9:00 A.M. until 4:00 P.M. There were 22 planes in our squadron, but only 18 would actually fly the mission. We learned that our squadron's job would be to drop paratroopers at a large base hospital in the middle of the Cherbourg Peninsula in France. They were to hold the hospital so that when injured troops came up from the beach, they could be treated there instead of being flown back to England. During the briefing, we saw pictures of the countryside and distinguishing landmarks near where we were to drop the troops. The most important landmark was the Merderet River. We were told to drop west of the river, which would be close enough to the hospital to capture it. The drop would take place at night to provide maximum protection from enemy fire. Nine planes would actually drop paratroopers at the hospital. Each plane would carry 18 paratroopers, a total of 162 men who were to take the hospital. Ahead of them would be a unit of paratroopers that would set up signal flares around the drop zone. Approximately two minutes before our outfit would drop, the troops on the ground would light up a T of flares so the pilot could see the drop zone. It seemed well planned and straightforward enough to me.

Next, they showed us our equipment. We were given a packet of French money and a phrase card with helpful French phrases and their pronunciations. We were told to carry only the money, a watch, and our dog tags—no driver's license or other identification. They also gave each of us a packet of medical supplies, including a capsule of morphine to inject for pain, as well as bandages and first-aid supplies. And they told us what to do if our plane was shot down. "If you're shot down, you have a couple of options," the trainer promised. "You can find a place to hole up—a barn or field—and hide out until the Americans come in. Or, if you want, you can try to join up with the paratroopers on the ground and fight. Either way is okay. Just realize that the Americans will come and take over. That's the whole point of the invasion." That, at least, was reassuring, even if the idea of being shot down wasn't.

My assignment was to fly the backup plane. I wasn't actually scheduled to fly in the invasion, but I had to be ready so if any of the planes didn't start or anything else went wrong, the paratroopers would race to my plane, and I would join the mission.

We were then given headings for the flight and strict instructions for takeoff. I, of course, had to know all this in case the backup plane was needed. There would be 72 airplanes flying out, four squadrons of 18 planes each. We practiced taking off so that half a group left from one runway, and just as the last plane passed the middle of that runway, another group would take off in a crisscross pattern until all 72 were in the air. It was timed to take only two and one-half minutes from the time the first airplane started to roll until the last one was off the ground—all 72 planes.

At 4:00 P.M., the briefing was over, and we went to dinner, filled with nervous excitement. But right after dinner, an officer came in and announced, "The invasion has been cancelled. The weather in France is too bad to fly in. But we all need to stand by. D-Day may be rescheduled at any time." In a way, this announcement only heightened the tension; I mean, we were ready to go, and now we had to wait again. But we all went back to playing cards and pretending it didn't matter. Of course, some of the talk drifted back to the afternoon's briefing. Suddenly, one of the paratroopers at our table, a new kid, burst out, "Hell, this is scary."

"Why?" I asked him. "You're just going to jump—exactly like we've done a million times in practice." I was scared, too, but I didn't want to show it. It wasn't like any of us had any experience. We were all kids. We *had* no experience with war. In fact, 80 percent of the paratroopers who were scheduled to jump on D-Day had never jumped in combat. But we couldn't let it get to us.

Then, a little incident happened that had a direct bearing on my status. As usual, I was playing blackjack after dinner when the squadron commander came in and interrupted the game. "Edwards," he said without preamble. "We've had a change of plan. After dinner, one of the pilots was goofing around, riding a bicycle with a nurse on the handlebars. He fell off and broke his arm. You'll be taking his place in the invasion." Suddenly, I wasn't flying backup anymore. I would be flying the mission to Normandy on D-Day.

Chapter Two

D-Day

D-Day

June 6,1944, will forever be known as D-Day, the beginning of Operation Overlord, the Allied invasion of German-occupied France. This huge war effort involved moving 175,000 men and their equipment, 50,000 vehicles including motorcycles, tanks and armored bulldozers, 5,333 ships and watercraft, and 11,000 airplanes across one hundred miles of water from England to occupied France in the dead of night. The surprise attack came after two years of careful planning and cooperation between the United States, France, and Great Britain.

The D-Day invasion involved four airborne divisions: the British 1st and 6th and the U.S. 82nd and 101st. The operation began with a dangerous attack by American paratroopers. Leaving from the English coast, they were to be dropped on the Cherbourg Peninsula to prepare the way for the amphibious troops that followed. The job of the 101st Airborne was to secure the western end behind Utah Beach and head off a German advance from the east. The 82nd was dropped further inland to secure the bridges and halt an advance from the west.

The planes were met with heavy fog and German antiaircraft fire, causing them to lose formation and scatter, unable to drop the paratroopers precisely as planned. The losses were heavy. Only one-sixth of the men in the 101st reached their destination points. While the 82nd fared better, they suffered heavy supply losses and were left with insufficient arms. However, the troopers on the ground managed to form smaller improvised squads and waged a fight, capturing St. Mere-Eglise that night.

Now, just 24 hours later, I was sitting in the cockpit of a C-47, copiloting one of the 18 planes that would fly over the Cherbourg Peninsula to drop 18 paratroopers into the combat zone in the dead of night. Today, we'd been given one last

England

Flight Pattern
for 82nd Airborne
on D-Day

160 Miles

North Sea

Grantham
Air Force Base

London

Exeter

English Channel

Map by Elizabeth Wick

briefing, going over the pictures of the jump zone one more time just to refresh the memory, then we were sent back to the barracks to wait it out. About 8:00 P.M., we came out to the planes. We were surprised to see that every plane had three white stripes painted on each wing and on the tail. "What are those stripes for?" someone asked. "It's for identification," we were told. "Every single plane that is flying tonight, bombers, gliders, paratroop drop planes, will all have the same exact stripes. That way, you won't be accidentally shot down by any of the Allies."

Then our group commander gave a last pep talk: "All right, boys, we're just going to go in, do our job, and come back home safely, if possible. Now, let's go get 'em!" We sang our squadron song, a lusty rendition of a little ditty about a pelican, our squadron emblem. All of it was designed to pump us up and give us courage. We were as ready as we could be.

They'd given us each a "flak suit," which was like a bulletproof vest. I decided to sit on mine, reasoning that any fire would come up from below, and therefore, it would protect my butt. Mechanically, I glanced around the plane, already so familiar to me. There were four seats total in the cockpit. As copilot, I sat in the front right seat. Bill, the pilot, was in the seat to my left. In front of us was the plane's instrument panel with its 1,400 buttons that could fly the plane automatically. Behind me sat Ring, the radio operator, and next to him, behind the pilot, was Henry, the navigator. Behind the cockpit, ranged along the sides of the plane, were benches where the 18 paratroopers sat, each weighing about 320 pounds with their gear and ammunition. In the back near the door was the crew chief, Roy Johnson, whose job was to make sure the paratroopers jumped at the proper time—even kicking them out of the plane, if necessary. From the ceiling in the middle of the plane hung a line that the paratroopers would hitch to before

C-47 controls

jumping. This cable would open the parachutes automatically and ensure an orderly jump. Underneath the plane, we had fastened what were called "belly jackets." These were bundles of supplies for the paratroopers. When the paratroopers jumped, the ninth one out would push a button at the back door that would release all the bundles. When they landed, the paratroopers would converge on the bundles and pick up additional arms before heading out on their mission.

We were scheduled to take off at 11:30 P.M. and make the drop in France at 2:30 A.M. In just three hours, if all went right, our part of the mission would be over, and we'd be heading back to England. Now, with just a few minutes left before takeoff, there was silence. There was no radio chatter; radio silence was not to be broken once we left the ground. There was to be nothing that would give away our presence. The tension in the plane was palpable, and I got that gnawing feeling inside, like my stomach was a pit full of spiders. The paratroopers sat in silence, with none of their usual good-humored ribbing of each other. They were nervous; only three of them had ever jumped in combat. One kid was chewing a piece of gum; harder and harder he chewed as his jaw got tighter and tighter. Someone attempted a rough joke, but no one laughed. We knew what was at stake. We were flying what was to be the biggest mission of the war. Our success could be the turning point.

Suddenly, all the waiting was over. The signal came, and we lined up on the runway, just as we had during practice. The night was clear as a bell, and a full moon was shining. It seemed like a sign from heaven. The last thing we heard before takeoff was our squadron commander's voice giving us the *sprag ho,* a standard procedure almost like a roll call. The radios were turned off; we would be in radio silence from that time on. Then the group commander in the lead plane gave it the gun and took off, and we all followed in the crisscross pattern with no more than 20 feet between airplanes. The only lights on the planes were special wing lights that couldn't

Paratroop Gear

Each paratrooper who jumped into combat carried an average of 70 pounds of equipment. Officers carried even more, averaging 90 pounds of gear. Adding in the parachute, most of the men carried 90–120 pounds over their body weight. Their gear included:

Standard Parachute Pack:
  M-1 Garand rifle with
    8-round clip
  Cartridge belt with canteen
  Hand grenades
  Parachute and pack
  Antiflash headgear and
    gloves
  Pocket compass
  Machete
  .45 caliber Colt automatic
    rifle
  Flares
  Message book

Spread throughout pockets:
  Loaded .45 automatic pistol
  Medical kit
  2 lbs. plastic high explosives
  Knife
  Bayonet
  Escape kit
  Toggle rope

Emergency Rations:
  4 pieces of chewing gum
  2 bouillon cubes
  2 Nescafe instant coffees
  2 sugar cubes, and creamer
  4 Hershey bars
  1 pack of Charms candy
  1 package of pipe tobacco
  1 bottle of water purification
    tablets

be seen from the top. They were pale blue lights that didn't radiate any light, but they were necessary for formation flying at night so you could tell how far you were from the other planes. Tonight the moon was so bright we didn't really need them.

As we started flying, we realized we were following the same course we had flown less than a week before when we'd done our dummy drop—same course, same headings, same timings, everything. It was a quiet flight; nobody said much; we were all bound up and nervous. We flew at about one thousand feet over England, and then dropped down over the water when we hit the coast. The only thing we spotted were two marker destroyers that sent up a signal to let us know that we were on the right path.

We flew south until we reached Jersey and Guernsey Islands off the coast of France, just west of the Cherbourg Peninsula. Our orders were to fly directly between the islands. The whole group flew in, one plane after another, low; we were flying in at about 150 feet. We drew antiaircraft fire from both islands, but all of it fell short of the plane. As we came in to the Cherbourg Peninsula, we saw light clouds ahead. Then, as we hit the coast, light arms fire from the ground peppered the plane. It was real light, maybe just .30-caliber rifles; it didn't feel dangerous. But suddenly a .50-caliber shot smashed into us, rocking the plane. I think it broke one of the rudder hinges because we had a heck of a time maintaining course after that. Just as we were back in position with the rest of the squadron, we ran into a fog bank. "Damn. The Germans must have sent up this fog bank to cause trouble. There's no way we can fly formation in a fog bank," Bill said grimly. All 18 planes scattered. We were on our own.

"Wish I knew what happened to the others," Bill commented tightly. "Keep an eye out for planes—we sure as hell don't want a mid-air collision!"

I nodded, peering out the front window. We were real low at this time, so I could see the landmarks. I knew that our drop point was off to the south a little bit, so we pulled up to six hundred feet where we were barely on top of this bank of fog and smoke. I was looking for the signal flares that the first paratroopers were supposed to have set up around the drop zone. But there were none. We later learned that the group of paratroopers who were to guide us in had all been killed on the ground. We had no flares. We had no formation. The only thing we could go by were the headings. We set the gyrocompass and kept our eyes peeled for landmarks. We knew we were getting close.

"We're three minutes from the drop zone," the crew chief called out. More enemy fire, heavier this time, rocked the plane. Outside, we could see enemy tracers lighting up the sky in arcs of color like the Fourth of July. Suddenly an explosion pounded our ears. There was a scream from the cabin. "We've been hit! Injuries in back." Just like that, one of the paratroopers was dead and another one injured. The injured one was a second lieutenant, the jump master, but he continued to call the mission. "We're two minutes from the drop zone." The remaining paratroopers by this time were hitched to the line and ready.

In front, Bill struggled to keep the plane aloft while I peered through the window looking for landmarks. The one thing they had impressed on us in the briefing was the river, how important it was to drop west of the river. They said if you came to a river and your troops weren't all out you should circle back and re-drop; no matter what, you had to go in there. I saw the river coming up and figured it was time. "One minute from the drop zone," Roy called. I pressed the button, which turned on a green light that signaled the paratroopers to jump. They started out one at a time, leaping into the night at six-second intervals despite the fire that continued to come up from the ground and pound the plane.

We had dropped by this time to about four hundred feet and slowed the airplane down to 110 or 115 mph, using half flaps. Pilots try to make it as easy as possible for the paratroopers because it's hard enough when the chute pops with a load like they were carrying, and the slower you can do it, the better it is for them. The chute pops automatically when it's released from the line, but each paratrooper carries an auxiliary chute. The minute he passes the tail of the plane, if his chute hasn't popped, he pulls the other one because he has only four hundred feet to get to the ground.

The troopers were jumping out one at a time; the ninth one pressed the button that would release the bundles, and then they were gone. I questioned the crew chief about the paratrooper who'd been shot. "Are you sure he's dead, or is there still a pulse? Will he need medical attention?" We needed to decide what to do next. But the paratrooper was dead, and the crew chief insisted there was nothing we could do. So we decided we'd just fly out to the east side of the peninsula, head out over the water and then north back to England.

We had only flown about a minute when a mobile unit on the ground opened up with 50-mm fire. The very first burst snapped the right engine, and our manifold pressure went down to the peg, which was nothing. With the plane rocking, I quickly feathered my engine, Bill gave the gun to the left, and we started to climb. "Everybody, put your chutes on," I shouted, not knowing what might happen next. On a hook in front of the navigator hung the two chutes for the pilot and copilot. Henry grabbed them both and handed them to us. Bill put his on, but I was too busy keeping the plane level, so I left mine off. The crew chief, Roy, came up front to be with the rest of us.

The guns kept firing, the sound deafening. We turned to the north to get away from them. We were picking up a little altitude, turning away, heading to the coast when all of a sudden an 88 outfit opened fire. An explosion rocked the cabin as a shell tore through the floor and opened up a hole just behind my seat. "My God," Henry screamed, "Ring's dead." Just like that, our radio operator was dead and the crew chief was injured, too. Ack-ack was pounding the aircraft like hail, the plane shook, and Bill and I were fighting with the controls, trying to keep it level. But it was no use. Another shell hit the remaining engine. I saw the manifold pressure drop, and I hit the bell to bail out. "Bail out; it's bail-out time," I yelled, and we all headed for the back door.

I had to scramble for my chest pack, but I found it and snapped it on, leaving my flak suit on the seat behind me. I turned around and straightened the airplane level again as the rest of the crew bailed out. Then I ran for the back door just ahead of the pilot. As the crew chief stepped out, a bright whirl of fire tore past the door, hitting him in the head, but he jumped anyway.

I hesitated at the door; I couldn't help it. All that fire was coming up. I could see the tracers, bright as the Fourth of July. Then I realized I still wore my earphone set under my overseas cap. I grabbed the cap and stuck it in my pocket, thinking I might need it later. I knocked off the earphones and took the plunge. As I passed the tail of the plane, I pulled the cord on my chute. It opened, and one second later I was on the ground. I had jumped from only about 150 feet. I thought I was a goner all the way, but when I hit the ground, I fell over, unhurt except for a twisted ankle.

When I opened my eyes, I saw that I was in an orchard; I'd landed between two trees. My first thought was that I was lucky I hadn't hit a tree and broken an arm or leg; with my second thought, I remembered my training. "Bury the chute," we'd been told. I struggled out of the heavy parachute. But I could still hear fire and see the tracers. I figured there wasn't time to bury it, so I just left it and ran in the opposite direction from the fire.

I ran without thinking, adrenaline pumping, for about two miles. Then, with a stitch in my side and the sound of gunfire behind me, I stopped for a minute to rest. I saw a path leading out of the orchard and I took it, this time walking and looking around for a house or barn where I could hide. Finally, I came to a dirt road that led to a house. I knocked on the door, but no one answered, so I went into the barn, climbed up to the hayloft, and sat down to collect my thoughts.

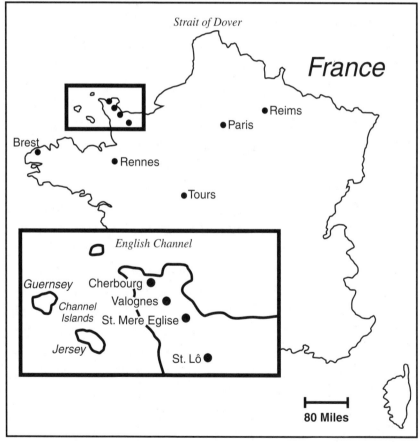

Map by Elizabeth Wick

Chapter Three

The Paratroopers

I sat in the hayloft assessing my situation. I was okay physically. My ankle hurt, and I was out of breath, but other than that I felt fine. I needed time to think. Until now I'd had no chance to think about anything that had happened. Had our mission been a success or a failure? The paratroopers had been dropped, but we'd lost the plane. Had I done everything I could to save it? I knew for sure that two of our crew had been killed: Ring, the radio operator, and one of the paratroopers. At least I assumed they were dead; I hadn't actually checked their bodies. Should I have checked? In all the commotion, had anyone checked for sure that Ring was dead? What could we have done if he wasn't? Why hadn't we all been killed when that shell exploded right behind my seat? Why was I still alive? The questions rolled through my brain as I replayed the scene in my mind. I didn't know if the others in the crew had survived their hasty jumps; I hadn't seen anyone since I'd dropped. No one in the world knew where I was right now. I had a .45 and the "clicker" they'd given us, a little hand-held device that sounds like a cricket when you click it together, which was supposed to help us find our fellow soldiers in battle. Other than that, I had nothing. No identification. They had stressed that we should carry no identification in case the Germans captured us. I felt utterly alone.

I thought about Ring. Out of all the crew, I knew him the best. He was the best radio operator in the whole squadron. While we were in England, we were supposed to go to Morse code training every week. I hated it, and when I tried to get out of it, Ring would always volunteer to take my place. "Sure, Stan," he'd say. "You've got enough on your hands with being the weather operator and doing the instrument checks. I'll go for you and sign your name." He was great at it, too. He could take 25 words a minute; I could only do about 12. Goodbye, Pal, I thought now, I'm sorry you didn't make it.

I thought about Shirley, too. My girlfriend, Shirley Broecker. Was she thinking about me right now? Was she wondering where I was? She didn't even know I was on this mission, since everything about the invasion had to be kept secret. I pulled out the small picture of her that I kept in my back pocket and stared at it, her quiet, intelligent face smiling at me, and I remembered the first time we'd met. It was in an English class in college, and I was sitting right behind her. Her long, brown hair fell over the top of her chair, and I thought it was the most beautiful thing I had ever seen. I thought of some trivial question and tapped her on the back. When she turned around, I fell in love. This is the girl I'm going to marry, I decided. The girl with the most beautiful hair in the world. I was still sure of that. I just didn't know when it would be. Shirley, I thought then, think of me tonight. Pray that I get through this okay and come back to you.

What should I do? I wondered. What should my next step be? I thought back to the briefing we'd been given (was it just two days ago?). "You can find a place to hole up and wait to be rescued, or you can try to join up with the paratroopers on the ground and fight." Should I wait until dawn and try to talk to the farmer? But what if he was a collaborator? Would he turn me in?

Outside, I could hear the sounds of battle, planes flying overhead and bursts of machine-gun fire. I sat there for about half an hour, too wired to sleep. Suddenly, I realized that I couldn't sit there any longer. I couldn't stand doing nothing—

hiding out while all those people were out there fighting. I decided I would walk back along the path and see if I could find any of the paratroopers.

So I climbed out of the hayloft and started back down the dirt path. It was about 3:30 A.M., and the night was dark. I had no idea where I was or where anyone else was. Suddenly, a shot rang out. I hit the dirt, and pulled out my .45. But what could I do with it? I was in a panic. Was it the enemy or our own troops? The only way to find out was to call the password, but my mind had gone blank. I couldn't remember it.

Finally, I remembered the alternative password, and I shouted out, "Thunder! Thunder, thunder," at the same time clicking the little tin clicker. Much to my relief, I heard the answering call, "Lightning." I was so relieved; it was our own troops. I walked toward the sound of their clickers, and seven paratroopers emerged from the darkness. None of them was familiar to me; there was a first lieutenant, a second lieutenant, and five enlisted men. I told them what had happened. "Similar story," the first lieutenant responded. "We were supposed to be dropped in St. Mere Eglise, but our plane got shot up coming over the coast and we were dropped off course. We need to get back there with the rest of our boys and help out. I don't know where your outfit is, so you may as well hitch up with us."

One of the paratroopers carried a BAR, a Browning Automatic Rifle, which is an extremely powerful machine gun that can shoot accurately up to half a mile or more. He was a short man, lean and sinewy, and looking tough as nails. Obviously a man of few words, he simply nodded at me, then paced back and forth on the path, anxious to move on.

Another of the paratroopers handed me a Thompson submachine gun. "Here," he said. "Take this. Know how it works?"

"Yes," I responded, "I've been trained." It was true; I had learned to use a Thompson as part of the special mission

The Paratroopers

Every paratrooper enlisted for the D-Day mission was a volunteer, and had been through rigorous training procedures. The paratroopers were in excellent physical condition, expertly trained in rifles and small arms, as well as jumping. In addition, they were highly motivated, and had bonded during their training into cohesive units. However, despite their training, they were not all experienced. In fact, only 20 percent of the paratroopers had ever jumped in combat. What they lacked in experience, however, they made up in spirit. As a rule, paratroopers tended to be confident, tough, and daring, willing to risk everything for the success of the mission.

The first paratroopers out were called Pathfinders, preceding the main troops by an hour or two. They were to mark the drop zones with automatic direction-finder radios and the Eureka/Rebecca Radar Beacon System (weighing 65 pounds), which could send a signal up to the lead C-47 in each flight. They would also mark the site with Holophane lights that formed T's on the ground. However, on D-Day, a cloud bank forced the pilots to climb above or fly below it, and antiaircraft fire forced the pilots to take evasive action. As a result, the planes were off-course, and the Pathfinders jumped from too high or low an altitude. As a result, only one of the eighteen American Pathfinder teams landed where it was expected to.

training I'd attended in April. I still doubted whether I would ever be able to kill someone, but I didn't tell him that.

"Good," the paratrooper replied. "Don't hesitate to use it. This is a war. It's kill or be killed."

The first lieutenant stepped in at this point. "This is my fifth jump in combat, and after this is over, I want to go home. There's no German who's going to stop me from doing that, and nothing I won't do to make sure I get out of this alive. Do you understand?"

"Right," I answered, sounding a lot more sure than I felt. I had no idea how I would react if I met up with a German. I hadn't expected to be fighting—just flying. How much different this was turning out than I had expected! I should have been back in England by now.

We walked cautiously along the path between the hedgerows. In this part of France, each field was marked by tall hedgerows, which consisted of a mound of dirt about four feet high, with a thick hedge of bushes planted on top of that. As we walked, we talked, telling our stories. I learned that all seven of these men were experienced paratroopers. Three of them had jumped together in Africa when the Allies had first invaded there. The first lieutenant and second lieutenant were friends who'd jumped together from Africa to Sicily and now to Cherbourg. One of them was from Washington State, the other was from Wyoming, and they were talking about getting together once the war was over. They just couldn't wait to get home again. It had already been a long war for them. I was glad to hitch up with guys who were so experienced. I was to learn in the next few days just how lucky I was!

It was beginning to get light when we came to a cross-road. "Stop," the first lieutenant cautioned. "The Germans probably have gun positions set up here to guard the cross-roads. We need to test it out before we try to cross."

"I'll go first to see if we draw fire," one of the enlisted men volunteered. "If not, you come across. If they fire, we'll have to dive through the hedgerows."

He started running across the intersection, and made it without incident. Next, the BAR man started across. Just as we thought he'd made it, there was a burst of machine gun fire. He took a last sprint, threw his gun over the hedgerow and dove after it. He'd made it; he hadn't been hit, but now the enemy was watching. We talked. "We have to cross that road to get to St. Mere Eglise," the first lieutenant instructed. "There's no way to set up a defense position from where we are, so we'll each have to make a dash for it."

And that's what we did. One at a time, at intervals, we each took a run and then jumped across the hedgerow. When it was my turn, I thought I'd never make it; that hedgerow looked a mile high. But I threw the Thompson over the top and then took a headlong dive right over the top of the bushes. All my training came back to me in a rush and I vaulted over the top; it even felt easy. Training is a funny thing. When you're being trained, it feels like just an exercise—you never really think about needing to use it. But it becomes part of you, and when you need it, it comes back in a rush, and everything you learned becomes automatic. I was to realize that over and over in the days ahead and thank the army for doing such a thorough job.

We all made it over those hedgerows, even with the Germans shooting from behind. Once over, the view from behind the hedgerows was a whole different story. Now we were on top, the ideal spot to set up a defense position, according to the first lieutenant. We all squatted down behind the bushes and fired back a bit, but then the first lieutenant said he had a better idea. "With a little strategy, we can take this unit out," he declared. "Look. I'll go one way, and George"—he pointed to one of the paratroopers—"you go the other way. The rest of you stay up here and keep firing for 10 minutes to distract them." So they left, the first lieutenant carrying a burp gun and the other fellow carrying a carbine. They skirted around the hedgerow on either side while we kept firing. After 10 minutes, we quit firing, and the next thing we knew we heard the burp gun going off. You can definitely tell the difference between an American burp gun and a German machine gun. We were grinning; it sounded like the plan was working.

Soon they were back, giving the thumbs-up sign. "We did it; there were four of them, and they're all dead." We ran down there and looked at the four Germans lying lifeless in the road. "Hurry up," the lieutenant cautioned. "We don't have much time." One of the guys wanted to take their guns, but another one disagreed. "It's better not to. If the Germans catch you with one of these guns, they'll know you killed somebody. It's better to leave everything as it is. Don't touch anything."

So we left and continued working our way up the road, using the hedgerows as cover. It was about seven o'clock in the morning by this time, and the sun was up, so it was becoming more dangerous to walk along the road because we were likely to run into German patrols. Finally we passed a cornfield, and we decided to go in there and sleep. Everybody was pretty tired. The paratroopers had been carrying all their equipment and guns, and it was heavy. They had K-rations with them, so we ate those, and we found a little stream and purified some water with the little pills we'd been given. Finally, we lay down in the corn rows and slept until dark. Then we set off down the road again and walked all night.

Chapter Four

Captured

The next morning we decided to stop at a farmhouse to see if we could get something to eat, and maybe find out what was going on. The first lieutenant spoke some French, which he'd learned in Africa. He didn't know a lot, but was able to make himself understood. We went down a little two-lane road and found a farmhouse set off the road about 50 feet; there was a big lawn between the house and the road. Two of the guys walked up to the door and knocked while the rest of us stayed back, ready to run.

A Frenchman answered the door. He was very friendly, and the lieutenant asked if he could give us some food. We said we could pay for it; we had all this French money that we'd been given before the invasion. *"Oui, oui,"* the farmer answered wholeheartedly and beckoned for us to come in. He opened a bottle of wine and gave us bread and ham and some ersatz coffee, which was really mostly milk. He was alone there, he explained, his wife and two children had gone off visiting for a few days, so he welcomed the company. Then he fried up some steaks, explaining that he'd slaughtered a cow just a few days before. The fellas paid him a good sum of money, the first lieutenant negotiating the price in his broken French, even though the farmer insisted that he didn't need to be paid.

We took off our shoes and socks, which were wet since it had rained a little the night before. It was odd, I hadn't really noticed the rain until I took my socks off and realized they were wet. It felt so good to sit down in a chair and put my feet up in front of the fire, drinking the strange coffee, which wasn't very good, but was so wonderfully warm! The Frenchman had a radio in the kitchen, and we listened to the news. We were horrified to hear that hundreds of Allied boats had been sunk at Omaha beach, and many soldiers drowned or were shot down. It sounded like the whole invasion had been a failure! I felt terrible for those men, but at the same time, I felt very lucky just to be alive.

When the steaks were done, the Frenchman invited us to the table. I got up, but one of the guys pointed to my shoes, still setting by the fire. "Better put those shoes and socks back on," he cautioned. "You never know what might happen." Reluctantly, I put them back on and sat down to eat.

I had just taken the first bite when we heard the skidding of brakes. Looking out the window, we saw that a German recon car had stopped right in front of the farmhouse. Again, training took over as we all jumped up, grabbed our guns and started to run. Each of us ran in a different direction inside the house until the lieutenant hissed, "Stand fast. Don't go anywhere!" So we each took up a position, trying to stay hidden. The BAR man left the house by the back door and went around to the side. I left the kitchen and hid behind some furniture in the living room. From there, I could see the men in the German car; their uniforms indicated that one was a general and another an *Oberleutnant*, equivalent to our first lieutenant, as well as a staff sergeant who sat in the backseat. Only three, but they were very high-ranking German officers.

Again, our first lieutenant made a decision. "There are only three of them. I'm going to see if I can tell what's going on." He stepped out on the front porch of the farmhouse with his burp gun and shouted in English, "Surrender. We've got this place covered!"

The driver's side of the car was facing the farmhouse, and the *Oberleutnant* stepped out and opened the door for the general. Then the staff sergeant got out on the other side. As he stepped out, he pulled his gun. Immediately, there was a burst of fire from the BAR, and the German staff sergeant lay on the ground, cut in two. The other two Germans put up their hands. The rest of us surrounded them, guns drawn. Four of us stayed behind to dispose of the body and pull the German car into the barn, thinking maybe we could use it to escape. I tried not to think about what I was doing as we lifted the bloody corpse and threw it over the fence. This was what it meant to "kill or be killed."

The others took the Germans into the house and tied their hands behind them to the chairs. When we returned to the kitchen, they had been separated and the first lieutenant was interrogating them one at a time, speaking in English. The general sat ramrod straight and answered haughtily, "Ze Germans vill vin this var, you know. Hitler has a secret veapon, vich you know nossing about."

"Shut up," the lieutenant responded. "Just answer my questions. Your job is just to answer the questions, if you want to stay alive." Then he asked him all kinds of military questions, about positions and so forth. This went on for about an hour, while the rest of us made sandwiches of the steaks and bread and drank some of the wine. We were feeling pretty secure.

Suddenly, there was the sound of trucks on the road outside. One of the paratroopers looked out the window and screamed, "Oh my God! It looks like the whole German army is coming up this road!"

"We'd better get out of here," the first lieutenant responded. "Run—run as fast as you can and get as far away from this place as possible."

We all grabbed our guns and tore out the back door, heading for the fields beyond. The Germans pulled their cars and trucks into the driveway of the house—they must have been planning to use it for a command post—and climbed out. One of them spotted us and shouted, and they pulled their guns and came after us, shooting.

We ran through the farmer's back field for about two hundred yards, and then we saw that behind it was a stream about four feet wide, and beyond that a steep embankment that went straight up about six feet. When I saw that hill, I thought I was dead. But we threw our equipment across the stream and leaped across, then scaled the embankment, grabbing hold of some little bushes that grew there. At the top, we took off again. We ran as fast as we could, at least five miles, dodging German bullets the whole way. Finally we came to an orchard, and we stopped running because we were dead tired; we couldn't run anymore. Then we saw that there were Germans on the road on the other side of the orchard, too. We were cornered.

"Maybe we can make a stand," the first lieutenant panted. We pulled out our guns and started to return their fire. I was busy shooting when all of a sudden I heard the lieutenant shout, "Behind you!" Instinctively, I snapped around and saw a German pointing his gun right at me. I shot without thinking, and saw him drop to the ground. Relief and revulsion ripped through me in equal measures; until now, I hadn't seen the result of my shots. But I didn't have time to reflect on it. Staying alive meant continuing to fire.

It wasn't long until the Germans upped the ante, throwing light mortar fire into the orchard. As it hit the ground, it spattered and burned, but luckily none of us were hit. "I don't know, boys," the lieutenant spoke. "We can make a stand and keep fighting 'til we all die, or we can give up and hope to escape later."

"Let's take a vote," one of the guys volunteered. "Who wants to give up?"

My hand went up, and so did the first lieutenant's. He'd meant it, I guess, about wanting to go home, no matter what.

Other hands went up, one at a time, until even the BAR man agreed. One of them grabbed a white handkerchief from his pack and began to wave it. As they surrounded us, we put our guns away and our hands in the air.

There was a lot of talk going on in German. I guess they were trying to decide what to do with us because by this time we were about five miles from the farmhouse and all of their vehicles. Finally, they commandeered a big recon truck from some of the soldiers on the road, put us in it, and three German soldiers drove us on up the road to Valognes. Even then, the lieutenant asked, "Do you think we should try to jump off?" But we decided not to risk it; they were watching us pretty close.

As we jounced along the road, I kept thinking how lucky it was that they hadn't decided to take us back to the farmhouse. They had never been inside. They didn't know we had killed a staff sergeant and tied up a general. If they'd found out, they would certainly have lined us up against the barn and shot us without a second thought. It seemed as if we had escaped with our lives, if not with our freedom.

Chapter Five

Two Escapes

We were taken to Valognes and put into a stockade with about 50 other paratroopers and infantry that the Germans had captured during the night. All day they added prisoners to the stockade until there were about one hundred of us. The prisoners wandered around talking to each other, while the Germans marched back and forth guarding us.

As the day wore on, I wandered away from the men I'd been captured with and talked to some of the other prisoners. Most of them were paratroopers whose planes had been shot down like ours, but there were some infantrymen there, too, who'd been captured near the beaches. Suddenly in the crowd I spotted a familiar face: Roy, the crew chief from our plane. "Hey, Roy," I shouted, "it's me, Stan." He turned and we embraced. We talked nonstop, going over what had happened since the plane was shot down. I was full of questions. "Gosh, it's good to see you. I saw that antiaircraft fire come up as you were jumping out, and I was afraid you were dead."

"Yeah, well, it hit me, all right." He pointed to the right side of his head at a large red crease just above his ear. "Luckily, it just grazed the side of my head; I never lost consciousness. But it was bleeding pretty badly and I felt woozy when I landed."

"What did you do?" I asked, remembering my own two-mile run down the road.

"Well, I didn't go far," he answered. "Right there where I landed, they had a battalion of 21 antiaircraft guns set up on

34

the ground. They had been shooting at us from there. The place was swarming with Germans, and I was captured immediately. I was almost glad, though, you know. I couldn't have run anywhere with that head wound, and they did give me medical attention."

"They did?" I asked, surprised.

"Oh, yeah, they patched me up pretty good, and then moved me here with some other prisoners."

"You're a miracle man," I marveled. "Hit twice before you even jumped, and still alive to talk about it."

"Yes," he agreed. "God was with me."

"You know," I said, "I can't stop thinking about Ring. Are you sure he was dead? I mean, everything was happening so fast, I never even had time to check."

"No, Stan, he was dead," Roy assured me. "I checked his neck for a pulse, but there was none."

We were silent for a minute, and then I spoke again. "I guess that makes me feel better," I said. "I just couldn't stand the idea that we might have left him alive in there to crash with the plane."

"I know," Roy answered. "But there wasn't anything we could do."

"Have you seen anyone else from our crew?" I asked.

"Not a soul," he replied. "As far as I can tell, we're the only ones that have been captured. At least so far."

We hung out for a while, meeting other prisoners as they came in and hearing their stories. We were pretty hopeful that we'd be rescued before long—after all, the Allies were making their presence known with bombs and strafing. It seemed that the Germans were in a state of confusion. All day long, the sky was filled with American A-20 twin-engine bombers, about forty of them that flew noisily overhead, dropping bombs. We prisoners couldn't tell what they were hitting, but we could hear the explosions and the roar of the planes. Some of the prisoners who understood German overheard the guards talking about what was going on. In this way, we learned that the Allies had bombed the railroad section of town and a couple of highway bridges going over a river.

That night the Germans gave us a little hardtack and we slept on the ground inside the enclosure. Luckily, it didn't rain because there was nothing to cover us. The second day we were moved by train to some little town north of Valognes. The train stopped at the station because the tracks had been bombed south of there. They broke us up into smaller groups, and moved us to different farmers' barns in the area. During this move, we lost track of some of the paratroopers we'd come with, and somehow I lost track of Roy again, too.

That night it was cold in the barn, and we slept together in groups of three or four. We took turns sleeping in the middle because that was the warmest place. Of course, we had no blankets or anything. While we were there, I bunked down with the two paratroop lieutenants, whose names were Jim and Lou, and we talked a lot about escaping. Even though they'd taken our weapons and packs when we'd been captured, these guys still had a lot of useful stuff sewn into the linings of their jackets, and they were pretty resourceful fellows. The whole time we were there, we watched for opportunities to escape.

The next morning, they piled us onto trucks headed north toward Cherbourg. As we neared our destination, the Germans made us all get out and march into town, displaying their prisoners. The French lined up on the street to watch, spitting at us and calling us names to impress the German soldiers who had occupied their town for the better part of the last three years. We ignored them, staring stonily ahead, but it was a strange feeling to be so reviled by people we'd supposedly come to help.

Eventually we reached the destination the Germans had in mind, a prison camp they'd set up in Cherbourg. It was a wire enclosure that had little one-story barracks with triple-decker bunk beds and straw mattresses full of fleas and lice. It was pretty disgusting. We stayed there for two days with about two hundred other prisoners. Our captors gave us as little to eat as they could get away with. There was just a small bread ration, and some watery barley soup.

After a couple of days, the Germans moved us again, loading us on trucks and heading down a country road bounded by hedgerows. Quietly, we discussed the possibility of escape. "Look," said one of the lieutenants. "If this truck stops for any reason, we're going to jump out. Once you jump, Stan, just hit the ditch and leap over the hedgerow. Don't even hesitate." I looked at those hedgerows and wondered if we could do it. With the trucks so close to the ditch and the Germans guarding the trucks, there would be no room for error.

Just 15 minutes later, our opportunity came. American planes overhead had spotted the convoy of German trucks and swooped low, strafing the area. The trucks stopped, and in the ensuing confusion, we jumped out, scaled the hedgerows without giving it a thought, and ran for freedom. They never even missed us. Once again, my training proved sound. We moved carefully cross-country to the east, toward the sound of battle, thrilled to be free again.

The next morning near dawn, after walking all night, we were feeling sleepy and looking for a place to stop when we heard shouts in German. "*Halt!* Stop!" Alarmed, we realized we had wandered too close to a large bivouac of sleeping German soldiers whose sentries had spotted us. We ran back in the direction we'd come from, but by this time their camp was aroused. Before we knew it, we were being fired at by German machine pistols from all sides, and this time we had no guns to fire back. "It's hopeless," one of the lieutenants shouted. "Put up your hands."

So ended our short burst of freedom. We were recaptured and taken to another truck convoy full of prisoners heading who knew where? By this time, around mid-June, we'd lost complete track of the war—all we knew was that we wanted to rejoin the American troops, but the Germans kept moving us somewhere else.

Each time we moved they would get us all together, and the officers had to line up so they could take a roll call. They always counted the officers, but the enlisted men were just a faceless group. That night, we drove up to a big empty factory, and they herded us in. It had walls and a roof, but there was nothing inside it, not even a concrete floor, just asphalt. The Germans had very little food to give us, so they said we could go next door to a farmhouse and see if we could dicker for some food. One of the guys I was with had some German marks, so he walked over there and managed to buy some bread and half a pound of butter. Some of the other guys got eggs and cheese, and we had a meal of sorts.

The next day they moved us again. That night we stopped at a huge three-story French castle with towers on all four sides. It was set back from the road and protected by towering leafy trees. It would have been hard to see the castle from the air, so it was probably safe from bombing. Outside, there was a courtyard and servants' house and a big garage. It must have been a wealthy estate at one time, but there was no one living there now. No furniture, nothing.

One of the guards hollered, "Pick a room and lie down— this is where you're staying today." Someone asked if we could go outside to pee, and he said we could use the outhouse and the pump out there in the yard. But he warned us that they would be guarding us every minute.

"Come on," beckoned one of my buddies. "Let's try to get away from the crowd." Our little group of three climbed the dusty, winding stairs. As the other prisoners picked out bedrooms on each floor, we kept climbing up all the way to the peak of one of the towers. At the top of the stairs was a trap door that looked as if it would lead to an attic. We pushed it open and climbed into a little round turret.

There was a window in one wall, and one of the guys walked over and looked out. "Not too close to the bathroom," he joked.

"But nice and far from the guards," said the other, more seriously.

"Hey, do you think they might forget about us up here?" I asked.

"Maybe," one of the guys answered. "Especially if we give them some help."

"What do you mean, help?" I questioned.

"Well, you know how the Germans are so class conscious? When they do a roll call, they never count the enlisted men—just the officers."

I nodded; we had all noticed it and commented on it before.

"Well, maybe we can make that work for us. Here's what I'm thinking. We'll probably stay here until at least tomorrow night, and then they'll try to move us out again. When that time comes, this is what we'll do." We whispered together until we had the details of a plan worked out.

We slept up there that night, and in the morning we went down to mill around with the other prisoners. We spent most of our time talking to the enlisted men, discussing the roll call that would come before the Germans moved the prisoners out again. And we wandered all over the castle until we knew every exit and where it led. When we returned to the turret that afternoon, we were wearing the caps of regular enlisted men, and three enlisted men were wearing our caps—the ones with the bars that showed our officers' ranks. Three non-ranking GIs had agreed to stand in our places during roll call. (Officers' orders, you know!)

That night the order for roll call came, but we didn't go. We sat up in the tower quietly watching out the window. We saw everybody line up and saw the Germans counting the officers. About 9:00 P.M. we heard the shouts and commotion of everyone leaving, but still we sat, not moving or speaking in case someone was looking for us. We waited until there was no more noise, and then we waited another hour for good measure. Finally we cautiously opened the trap door and climbed down the back stairway. The place was deserted.

We left through a back entrance near a neighbor's field. Beyond that was a vegetable garden that we'd spotted that afternoon. This was our destination. Furtively, we entered the garden, and with some of the paratroopers' tools, we dug up potatoes, radishes, and green onions from the field. "Food!" we rejoiced. "Blessed food."

Free again, and with food in our pockets, we set out once again for the American lines.

Chapter Six

On the Loose

We moved that whole night, working our way east with the aid of a compass that one of the men had in his pack. We figured that the American line must be east; we could hear the sounds of battle in that direction. We thought that if we could get close to the line, we could hide until the Americans crossed the line, and then we could be repatriated.

We were feeling touchy—vulnerable. We were deeper than ever into German-held territory, we no longer had weapons, and by this time we all knew what it felt like to be captured. We knew, too, how many Germans were out there, and how easy it would be to get shot. We also knew that in order to get across to the American line we would have to cross the very thickest part of the battle. The paratroopers had been told that the Americans were planning to capture St. Lô, and we figured that if we could get there, we'd have a good chance of finding them. One of them had a map of the area, but it wasn't very useful because we weren't exactly sure where we were.

The best we could do was to keep walking south and east, hopefully toward St. Lô. We kept off the roads and traveled between the hedgerows, over fields, never on a path. That first night we walked about ten kilometers. As dawn approached, we could see that we mustn't travel by day; the place was loaded with Germans. But we found a cornfield and hunkered down beneath the sheltering green arms of the corn plants.

"Well," Lou declared. "Time for a little cribbage before we turn in." I stared incredulously as he produced a cribbage board and deck of cards from one of the voluminous pockets of his uniform, and he and Jim settled down to play. I was astonished that they could play cards at a time like this, but it wasn't long before they were teaching me the elements of the game. All day we played cribbage and took turns napping between the corn plants, while we watched the American fighter planes roaring overhead and tried to figure out what they were shooting at and how the war was going. By nightfall we were once again on the move.

Traveling this way was very slow. For one thing, the days in France at that time of year are long; it doesn't get really dark until about 11:00 P.M., and the sun is up again at 4:30. We had to be cautious; the hedgerows provided good cover, but they made it very difficult to see who or what was in the area. We never knew what might be lurking behind the next hedgerow.

We traveled this way for two days, moving at night, resting and watching by day, eating only what we could find in farmers' gardens. We had one canteen among the three of us, and we filled it with water from small streams or ponds and purified it with the little tablets. After two days we were relatively close—the sounds of battle fire and the explosions of mortar shells had grown louder and closer. But we were starving; all we'd had to eat for days were raw vegetables and water.

In this area there was a community of farms; the farmhouses were set near each other in a big circle with their fields spread out behind them. After walking all night in the rain, we were wet and cold and starving, and we decided to take a chance. So we went up to one of the houses and knocked on the door. The French farmer welcomed us in and introduced his wife and two young children who peeked out shyly from behind their mother. They seemed very glad to see us—welcomed us in, saying, "*Américain, américain.*" We sat on the floor in front of the fireplace and took off our shoes—what a relief! It had been days since I'd been able to take them off. The wife bustled around the kitchen and brought us bread and cheese and whatever else she could find. It seemed like word of our arrival had spread through the small community the minute we got there. Pretty soon neighbors showed up at the back door, wanting to talk to us. We had a hard time because none of us really spoke French, except for Jim's smattering and the inadequate phrases we could read off the phrase card we'd been given in training, things like "I am hungry," and "I need help." None of the farmers spoke English, either, but there was a lot of smiling and sign language and they'd jabber among themselves in French, though we had no idea what they were talking about.

They seemed really friendly, and we were just beginning to relax when a German truck came down the road. To me, it was déjà vu; once again I was warm and cozy in a French farmhouse when the Germans drove up and ruined it. Hastily, the farmer pushed us out the back door, and with sign language and French phrases told us to wait for him at the back of his property, where he would bring us food. We took off in the direction he pointed and spent the day in his cornfield while the Germans were in the house. About four o'clock in the afternoon, the farmer came down the corn rows bearing sandwiches and ersatz coffee. We thanked him profusely and showed him the map, trying to get an idea of where we were. We asked him what was the best way to get to St. Lô. He showed us, and pointed out places we should avoid where there were German encampments, saying, *"Non, non. Boche!"* We struggled to understand and remember.

Once it was dark, we moved on. In the early morning, about five o'clock, we stopped again. We had found a hill—really a wide mound of dirt about eight feet high and ten feet across the top with hedges all around the top. "That looks like a good place to hide for the day," one of the paratroopers declared.

"Yeah," the other agreed. "We'll be able to see what's going on."

So we climbed on top of this hill and hid behind the hedges. No one could see us, but if we stuck our heads out, we could survey the area. Right along the road were a couple of farmhouses. Emboldened by our last experience with a French farmer, we decided we'd wait until about seven o'clock, then knock on one of the doors and ask for food. As the light came up, I was ready to move. "Okay," I announced. "I'm going down there." Just then, the door of the farmhouse opened below, and a German soldier stepped out. "No, I'm not," I declared, and sat quickly back down. "I'm not going anywhere."

So we hid behind the hedges all day, and at night we moved on again in the direction of St. Lô. By morning we figured we were at most 10 miles from the front lines. It was no longer safe to sleep outdoors, but we found an out-of-the-way barn. There was a huge 500-gallon barrel of cider in there, and we opened the spigot and drank our fill. We sat inside waiting for daybreak, determined to ask for food. "I'll go to the door," I volunteered. I got out my paper with the French phrases and started to practice. "*Je suis américain*," I planned to say. "*J'ai faim*—I'm hungry. Can you help me?"

About six o'clock, we approached the house. As I went to the door, my two paratrooper buddies stood at each corner of the building, watching for danger. I knocked on the door, mentally rehearsing. It was a Dutch door, the kind where you can open the top to talk and leave the bottom closed for security. In a minute, the top door swung open, and a man stood there, naked to the waist. He looked sleepy and was chewing something. He wiped his mouth with the back of his hand and stared at me. "*Je suis américain*," I began—and then I saw his pants. He was wearing the gray pants of a German army officer.

In complete confusion and fear, I turned and shouted, "Let's get out of here!" and took off, my friends behind me. The

German ran out of the house in his bare feet, carrying a loaded gun, which he shot at our retreating forms. We tore through the winding alleys and side roads as fast as we could, bullets and fear propelling us through the narrow alleyways, aware that it was already too light to be moving around. We jogged off to another little side road so we wouldn't be seen.

"We'd better find a place to hide," I panted, stopping for a minute.

"There," one of the others pointed. "In the lilac bush."

I looked where he was pointing and saw a huge lilac bush, about twenty-five feet around with lots of leafy green foliage. I nodded. "That'll do. I don't see much else."

We climbed into the lilac bush, crouching in the crotch where all the branches started, about three feet off the ground. We tried to make ourselves comfortable by leaning into the big arms of the tree. Incredulously, I saw my buddies take out the cards and cribbage board and settle into the middle branches to play. How can they play cribbage at a time like this? I wondered. I sat a little farther out and strained to see between the leaves.

For about two hours we sat there like that, listening to the sounds of the battle and Allied planes going overhead, strafing the area. About ten o'clock two Germans came up the side road leading horses that pulled wooden wagons filled with supplies. They pulled them up under the shade of the trees, right next to where we were sitting. I held my breath, and looked at my friends in panic. They ignored me and went right on silently playing cribbage.

The Germans were talking with one another, pointing to the sky and sounding alarmed. Then one of them pointed to the lilac bush, talking a mile a minute in German. He pulled out a little axe and began to chop off the branches of the lilac bush. I watched in a state of near panic. What was he doing?

He handed the branches to the other fellow, who stuck them into the wooden slats of the wagon and nodded approvingly. Suddenly I understood. They were camouflaging the wagon with branches so it wouldn't stick out as a target for the Allied bombers. I watched in helpless horror as the man continued to chop branch after branch of our shelter away. I tried to catch the eyes of my buddies, but they just went on playing cribbage as if nothing was wrong. I didn't dare move— all I could do was watch and wonder how far he would go.

Finally, he started to tear away the inner branches just a foot from where I sat. He looked up and saw me staring down at him. Alarmed, he shouted something in German, dropped the axe and took off across the field, his friend right behind.

"Let's get out of here," I yelled, free of my enforced silence. The guys folded up their cards and we took off in the opposite direction from the Germans. In broad daylight we crossed this really big field, running like crazy men until we saw a barn at the back of the property. "In there," the lieutenant shouted, and we ducked inside.

The barn was not empty. As we entered, a French farmer turned around, abandoning whatever task he was performing.

"Can we hide in here?" we asked breathlessly.

His eyes filled with alarm. *"Non, non, non,"* he shouted in a panic. He made us understand that he couldn't hide us, it wasn't safe, that the whole area was infested with Germans, and they would kill him if he were caught hiding the enemy.

"Okay," we answered, not wanting to put him in danger. We sneaked out of the barn and headed for another one. Suddenly, there was a shout. Shots rang out, and we were surrounded by what seemed like fifty thousand Krauts hollering and screaming and pointing their guns.

There was nothing to do but put up our hands. Once again we were captives of the German army. I was angry and frustrated and hungry. We had come so close; it just seemed too cruel to be captured again. "Well," I asked the German officer who held me, "are you going to feed us at least? I'm hungry."

"*Nein,*" he answered. "No food. You're going to the CP [command post] to talk to the SS."

Chapter Seven

The Third Escape

The command post was housed in a nearby farmhouse that the Germans had taken over. They took us to a room upstairs for interrogation. The major in charge was a big, burly man who spoke excellent English and questioned us over and over, turning from one to the other of us without warning. "What is your name?" he barked at me.

"My name is Stanley Edwards; I'm a second lieutenant, serial number 0701914," I answered carefully. My palms were sweating. I didn't want to make a mistake. I knew that no matter what he asked, I could only tell him my name, rank, and serial number. That's what we'd been trained to do.

"What unit are you with?"

"My name is Stanley Edwards, second lieutenant, serial number 0701914."

He threw questions out as fast as we could answer, jumping from one to the other of us with lightning speed.

"How did you get into this country?" "My name is Stanley Edwards, second lieutenant, serial number 0701914." "How long have you been here?" "My name is Stanley Edwards, second lieutenant, serial number 0701914." "Where did you stay last night?" "My name is Stanley Edwards, second lieutenant, serial number 0701914." "When was your last meal?" "My name is Stanley Edwards, second lieutenant, serial number 0701914." And on and on.

Finally he got mad and pounded the table. "If you don't start answering questions, you'll get nothing to eat," he threatened.

"Too bad," one of the paratroopers answered. "That's all we're going to tell you." I winced, hoping he hadn't gone too far with his bravado. Even though I was really hungry, my worst fear wasn't that I'd get no food. My worst fear was that I'd be separated from my friends.

The interrogation wore on. No matter what the major asked, we told him only our names, ranks, and serial numbers. Eventually, he gave up in disgust. "Throw them in that room," he shouted to the guards.

At last it was over. The relief was stunning. They put us in a room and finally brought us some food: a bowl of barley soup, a chunk of blood sausage, a slice of bread, and a cup of mint tea. That tea was disgusting, but the food was welcome, and the best part was that we were still together.

The next day they moved the three of us down to a house that they had fixed up as a prison. There were eight or ten other Americans—infantry and tank guys that they had captured in various places on the peninsula—already imprisoned there. The prison looked just like an ordinary farmhouse except there were bars on all the windows. They put the three of us in the same room; it looked like a bedroom with a single cot, a dresser, a chair, and a fake fireplace. We looked it all over, and one of the paratroopers said, "Nah, we can't stay here. We're going to have to find a way to escape."

"Yeah," the other one chimed in. "We've come this far— we can't let a few bars stop us."

We went over to the window and shook the bars. They stayed firm. Peering out, we saw a Frenchwoman walking up the alley. "Madame," Jim called out. "*Nous avons faim. Avez vous quelque chose a manger?* Have you anything to eat?" I had no money—they had taken it away when they interrogated me. But the other two guys produced money that had been sewn into the linings of their jackets and dickered with the Frenchwoman.

"*Voilà*. Dinner," Jim grinned as he turned away from the window bearing a loaf of French bread.

"What else do you have in that lining?" I asked curiously as I watched him ripping the stitches out of his coat. He smiled as he proudly produced a small tool. It was grooved and sharp on the back and came to a sharp point on the front.

"I've got one, too," Lou added, proffering an identical tool.

I didn't get it. There was no way that little tool would cut the steel bars on the window or go through the bricks, and it wasn't big enough to threaten any German soldier with. "Watch and see," Jim promised. "This ought to do the trick." He began to scrape away the mortar around the window.

Suddenly I understood. We were going to try to remove the bars.

We took turns with the tedious work. Two could scrape while the other stood watch by the window. It was hard work, scraping and scraping with that little tool, but we kept at it. Sometimes we'd hear the Germans outside and were afraid they'd heard us, so we'd stop work. By dusk, we had scraped away enough that we could see the bottom of the bars. They were all attached together.

The lieutenant grabbed the bars and pulled hard. They moved the tiniest bit. "Yes," whispered Lou. "This is going to work!" Encouraged, we kept scraping, so intent on our work that we forgot to watch as carefully. All of a sudden, the door opened without warning and a German soldier walked in. We looked up guiltily. There was no hiding what we were doing. At this point, it was painfully obvious.

It was also obvious that we were going to have to do something about the soldier. The first lieutenant grabbed him from behind and pulled him into the room, at the same time covering his mouth. Without even thinking about it, I gave a quick karate chop to his neck. He stopped struggling, Jim let go of him, and he fell to the floor. But before I could breathe, he was up again. As he sort of shook himself, regaining his bearings,

I grabbed his head in a headlock and twisted hard. I heard his neck snap; then he went limp. He was dead.

"What do we do now?" I whispered fearfully, feeling sick.

"Quick," Jim answered. "The closet. We can put him there." We dragged the body to the closet and sort of folded him up on the floor.

"We've got to get out of here quick," Lou said. "Is the door open?"

We tried it, but it had swung shut and locked again.

"Nothing to do but to keep on scraping," Jim replied grimly. "We've got to work fast."

So we kept scraping, the dead soldier in the closet, while darkness gathered outside. When we had uncovered another third of the bars, we tested them again. This time they moved more easily. "Okay, yank!" Jim commanded. Straining, we all pulled as hard as we could. Suddenly the window gave way and we pulled it inside, bars and all. Cautiously we stuck our heads out and looked around. There was a guard in the front of the house, but there were none in the back. Squeezing through the empty window, we took off. Once again, we were free and out in the open.

We ran as fast as we dared, trying to put as much distance as possible between the Germans and us. We had a rough idea of where we were. Although they had moved us around some after they captured us, we hadn't been taken very far, and we still had the Frenchman's directions in our heads and the map in someone's hidden coat pocket. On the map we could see a place where two railroad tracks crossed, and we figured if we could find that spot, we could orient ourselves. We ran until we found the railroad tracks and then followed them until they crossed and we knew where we were. We began to move toward the battle.

We traveled as before, sleeping during the day, traveling at night, and eating whatever we could find. One night, it was nearing dawn when we came to a couple of barns. One appeared to house some cows—we could hear them lowing and moving around. The other, with half its roof blown off, seemed to be deserted. We decided to hide there for the day.

Carefully we entered the dusty interior. As our eyes adjusted to the darkness, we saw that there was a hayloft above filled with square bales of hay. "Up there," one of the paratroopers pointed. We found a ladder against the wall and carefully climbed to the loft above, shoving it down when we finished so no one would know we were there. The hay felt soft after the hard ground and the bales provided cover, and we sank down and slept for a couple of hours.

We were awakened by the sound of the barn door opening. I froze, straining to see in the dim light. Outlined against the light of the doorway was a teenage boy. He looked straight up to the hayloft, then got the ladder and climbed up. What the heck? I wondered. It was almost as if he knew we were there.

"Do not worry," he whispered in heavily accented English. "You are American soldiers, *non?*"

We nodded, still wondering how he knew about us. "I heard you come in during the night. My parents and I—we are sleeping in this barn"—he pointed to the space below—"because the Germans have taken over our house. They are using it for a command post."

My eyes widened at this, and beside me, one of the paratroopers instinctively reached for a weapon. "Where?" he whispered.

"The house is that way," the boy said pointing, "about one hundred meters. You must be very careful."

"Are we near St. Lô?" we asked.

"Very near," the boy answered. "St. Lô is about five kilometers away." We got out the map and he showed us where we were. Then he whispered, "I must go back. I am supposed to be feeding the cows. But wait here. My mother cooks for the

Germans. She is making cheese today, and I will bring you some."

Then he climbed down. We waited, now in a state of nervous tension. The barn no longer seemed so cozy, knowing that the Germans were quartered on the same property.

True to his word, though, the boy returned, bringing warm potato pancakes and bottles of cider. He passed them up to us through holes in the floor, and we discovered we were right above the place where his family was living in the barn. It was closed off from the main part of the barn, which was why we hadn't seen it when we came in the night before. We sat up in the loft and ravenously ate the food. Those potato pancakes were out of this world—I thought I had never eaten anything so good!

Later that evening after dinner, the boy's parents came back to the barn with him, bringing bread and cheese and good wishes. When the light faded, we said careful good-byes and moved out again. All night we could hear bombs and see flashes of explosions. We knew we were getting close.

Chapter Eight

Captured Again

The next night, we found the gate to a field. Like all the fields in France, hedges surrounded it. Preferring not to travel by road, we went through the gate and started cautiously crossing the field. We scarcely dared to breathe because we were so close to the front line. The night was so dark we could barely see each other, let alone where we were going. I was listening intently and peering through the darkness when I ran smack into something big and black and warm. The form shifted. I heard a loud "neigh" that almost startled me off my feet. I had run right into the side of a horse! Minutes later I heard a grunt and my buddy pushed me aside. Looking down, I saw a sleeping soldier. The field that we were traveling through was loaded with Germans. They were bivouacked there for the night. So we turned tail and ran as fast as we could back toward the gate, down the side of the hill, and over another hedgerow.

But we'd been spotted. Suddenly, the air was filled with shouts and gunfire, and before we knew what had happened, we were captured again. One of the German soldiers grabbed me from behind and pushed me roughly to the ground. There was some more talk among the soldiers, which we didn't understand, but the upshot was that the soldier who held me was to take us somewhere. They got us in a line, Lou first, Jim second, and me last, with the guard taking up the rear, and pointed us down this path. We were all frustrated, hungry, tired, and angry at having been captured, and the German guard's attitude didn't help much. He kept shoving his rifle into my back, and snarling, *"Raus, raus!"* which means move ahead or move on. It made me so angry, I just wanted to turn around and hit him. As we moved along on this narrow path, every few minutes I would feel that gun in my back and hear him shout, *"Raus!"* Suddenly, something inside me snapped. I leaned toward the first lieutenant, and muttered, "Do you want me to take him out?"

"Do you think you can?" he responded.

All I said was, *"Raus."*

The gun jabbed my back again, and I felt the anger leap inside me. With one swift move, I turned, grabbed the end of the rifle, took it out of the German's grasp, and slammed it into the side of his head. He went down, but he jumped up quickly, and this meant hand-to-hand. While Jim grabbed his rifle, I got a headlock on him, and with one quick squeeze, I broke his neck, just as I had been taught to do in commando school.

"Quick!" Lou urged. "Let's get out of here."

I had no time to think about what I had done, as we ran like crazy to get out of that area, once again leaving the gun because it would be too incriminating. It was such a dark night that we were disoriented. We seemed to be on a path on the other side of the hedgerow. We were running along when all of a sudden, the ground dropped off sharply about 20 feet. It was really strange. We saw a pile of straw there, so we jumped down into it, thinking it was a good place to hide and rest for a bit. We were breathing hard, not daring to talk. Suddenly, a dog started barking. It sounded as if the animal was right underneath us! We peered out from the straw into the drop-off. We couldn't see anything, but the animal kept barking below. "What the heck is going on?" I whispered. "How can there be a dog below us?"

"Shit," one of the guys exclaimed, suddenly getting it. "We're sitting on the straw roof of somebody's house!" Sure enough, this was a house built into the side of the hill. Now we could make out a bar running down the side like a conduit pipe. Quickly we shimmied down that and got to the lower ground. The dog kept barking and barking from inside the house, giving me a headache. We took off through that field, hoping against hope that the Germans wouldn't hear and decide to investigate.

We kept moving until dawn, when we came up to an old factory. They must have made bricks there at one time because bricks were piled all over the place. Cautiously, we entered the building and found a place to hide behind some of them. All day long we heard Germans outside the building marching up the road. Whenever there were Germans in the area, you knew it. They talked real loud and barked orders; they just acted like they were in control. There was no way we dared move out of the factory to look for food. We just hunkered down, listened to the Germans, and prayed they wouldn't find us.

From what we could tell on the map, we thought the American lines ran through the middle of a swamp just to the east of us. We figured that if we got into that swamp, we could probably work our way through it. That's where we would head come nightfall, we decided.

When night came, we left the brick factory and headed east. We kept cutting over hedgerows and roads, all the while dodging German outfits. We were so close we could almost taste freedom. But there were all these Germans in our way. At one point, we saw them stringing communication wires. They didn't bury them, just laid them across the road. We dodged back and hid behind the hedgerow. "What are they doing?" I whispered.

"Those are for close communication with the CP," the paratroopers told me. "It's a sign of how close we are. We need to be really careful, but we've got to get across that line."

We were hiding in the hedgerow, waiting for a better chance to get across when a German soldier emerged through the hedge, not three feet from us. We ducked down into the bushes, holding our breath and watching in horror. He set down his weapon, pulled down his pants and squatted. He was so close we could have grabbed his rifle, but we left him alone, not wanting to raise an alarm. Five minutes later, he finished his business and ducked back into the hedgerow, never suspecting we were there. We began to breathe again.

Near daybreak, we were cramped and hungry. "I'm starving," I complained. We hadn't had anything to eat since the boy had brought us food—almost two days ago. There was a light on in a nearby farmhouse. "Let's go over there and see if they'll give us something to eat," I begged.

Slowly, the lieutenant nodded, and we cautiously approached the house. I knocked and a Frenchman answered the door. *"J'ai faim,"* I said, my stock phrase. He answered with a torrent of French words and gestures, ignoring my repeated pleas for food. Finally, I turned to the other guys and complained, "Well, I don't understand this guy and he's not paying any attention to me, so what should we . . ."

Just then, the barn door opened and out stepped a couple of Germans, carrying their rifles. Recognition dawned. I stared at the Frenchman and watched him gesture helplessly as if to say, "I tried to tell you." The Germans were behind us in an instant. They did a double take, realized who we were; then their rifles snapped up, and they began uttering commands in staccato German. There was nothing we could do except put our hands up.

As they shoved us roughly toward a '35 Ford parked in front of the barn, my head was reeling. Dimly I noticed that the car was just like the one I had at home. But I had no time to wonder, I felt so deeply humiliated and discouraged. We had been so close! Why had I knocked on that door? How could we continue to escape, each time to be recaptured? And why was it that every farmhouse we stopped at was being used as a Nazi headquarters? Only that one time—the time the farmer treated us so well and brought us sandwiches—that was the only time we'd gotten away with it. I felt so depressed. Why had we kept on knocking on doors?

Of course I knew why. The need for food was overwhelming—it had become more important than anything else in the world—the lack of food was more of a threat than German weapons or American bombs. I knew I had lost at least 15 pounds since I'd been shot down—I was pulling my belt tighter every day, and it seemed harder and harder to summon the strength to walk every night. I had dreamed of being reunited with the American forces—dreamed of K-rations and coffee. Right now I hardly cared that we'd been captured again. I just hoped they would feed us.

But they didn't feed us. They took us to another farmhouse where the SS again interrogated us. This time they took us in one at a time and the SS officer in charge really raked me over the coals. I kept saying my name, rank, and serial number, but he paid no attention. There was a box of cigarettes on his desk. They were American cigarettes that he must have confiscated from some other prisoner. "If you talk to me, you can have one," he promised. Like the first interrogator, he spoke excellent English. This one seemed to know a lot about the United States. "You sound like you are from Chicago or St. Louis," he mused. I sensed that he was trying to trap me into revealing something about myself and steeled myself to be silent. My head hurt with the effort of trying to put him off, answering only with my name, rank, and serial number. Finally, trying to achieve an air of bravado, I reached for a cigarette from the box on his desk. With a flash of temper, he slammed the lid down and put the box in his drawer. *"Nein!"* he snapped. "Soldier, this war is over for you." And with that,

I was dismissed, my mind in turmoil. What did he mean, "It's over for you"? I suddenly felt very frightened and again wished fervently that I had never knocked on that last door!

After that interrogation, we were herded back into the Ford and driven south all the way to a town called Rennes, which is on an equal line with the Brest Peninsula. With every mile down the road, my hopes faded. We had been so close—how would we ever escape now?

Chapter Nine

In the Boxcar

Rennes was a major artery with a big prison camp housing about five hundred prisoners. The railroad line ran right through the center of the camp. When we arrived, it was around the first of July. We stayed in the camp all that day and the following day. While we were there, we learned that the Americans had made big inroads up north and were starting their push south. They were bombing and strafing Rennes because it was such an important transportation center. The Germans were returning ack-ack fire at the American planes. It was all very noisy and confusing. A group of prisoners were standing together talking when suddenly an antiaircraft shell that hadn't exploded came back down and landed right in the middle of these guys' conversation, exploding on impact. There was screaming and more commotion. It looked like about five of them were hurt. I ran over to the knot of injured soldiers and saw that one of them had suffered a direct hit. His thigh and groin were split completely open. I dove in without thinking and held the wound together, pressing hard to staunch the bleeding. Eventually, the Nazis came over and took the injured away—to the hospital, they said. I later learned that my efforts had done no good; he died later that night.

The next night, they removed us from the prison and put us into small wooden boxcars on the railroad track. There were 50 guys in each boxcar, 25 to a side. We sat there with our heads up against one wall and our feet sticking out straight in front of us. Heat rose quickly in the airless car and perspiration dripped from our bodies. Very little light penetrated the space from between the wooden slats on each side. The Germans put a 30-gallon drum in the middle of the car to use as a WC and slammed the door shut. The train began to move, heading south. We tried to watch through the spaces between the slats to see where we were going.

Hours later, the train was still moving, and someone had to use the waste drum. The stench rose and mingled with sweat and body odors.

"That thing is going to stink so bad, we're going to be sick," someone complained. "Maybe this will help," another guy offered, and put his jacket over it to cut the smell a little.

From the minute we got into that boxcar, everyone talked of escape. Not one of us was willing to simply lie down and take it! We discussed successful past escapes—several of the guys had stories to tell. There was a British soldier who'd

German Use of Railroad Cars

During the war, the Germans used railroad lines extensively for shipping prisoners. Jews and other "undesirables" from Germany and other European countries were deported to concentration camps by way of the railroads. Some of these camps were deliberately situated along major rail lines in Poland. Forty-four parallel tracks led to Auschwitz alone.

People were packed into ordinary freight cars under terrible conditions: 50-100 people per car with horrible sanitation, little food or water, and suffocating heat in summer or freezing temperatures in winter. Many of those deported died during the journey. These wooden boxcars had slats that allowed just a tad of light to enter, and sometimes a board would be broken or missing so that they could peer out. When they stopped at railroad crossings, prisoners would put their hands out of these slats and beg for help from whomever might be passing by.

Allied prisoners of war were also sent to prison camps in these wooden freight cars. It would appear that they were treated slightly better than their Jewish counterparts, being given a little food and water and allowed to empty the waste can each day. Still, their treatment was horrible, and many prisoners suffered terribly as a result.

been shot down in France and escaped three times before; he'd gotten back through the underground and had a rough idea where they might be contacted. Another fellow in the car was Colonel Good from the 29th Division. It drove him crazy to be a prisoner; he just wanted to be back with his men.

I quickly made friends with a Canadian named Norman Patrick Murphy who reminded me of a British fighter pilot I had known. He was a funny guy, always ready with a story to tell or a quip that made us laugh. When the Germans fed us that first day, they gave each of us a loaf of bread and warned, "Don't eat it all at once. This has to last you for three days." Norman Patrick Murphy immediately sat down and ate the entire loaf. "What are you doing?" I asked him. "You have to make that last for three days." "*I* may not last three days," he answered, "and then this bread would go to waste." And with that he finished off the loaf.

There were also several paratroopers who still had useful tools sewn into their jackets. About five of them pulled out hacksaw blades, and after much discussion, they decided to try to cut a hole into the side of the wooden boxcar. "We'll make it big enough to climb through and escape that way," they promised. But the work was slow, and the risks of detection were great. After they had cut several gashes into the wooden slats, someone had another suggestion. "Why not cut a hole in the door instead? This car is only fastened shut with wire; if we cut a hole in the door, we can just reach out, remove the wire, open the door and jump."

A cheer went up from the guys in the car. This was a plan that just might work. By the next day, a hole big enough for a man's hand was cut next to the door handle. Several of the guys donated chewing gum to hold the wood in place until the hole was needed, and plans for escape were made. We would have to jump while the train was moving, but that seemed possible as it often slowed to about 25 miles per hour. "We'll jump out in groups of three or four," we decided, "and we'll draw straws to see who goes first." We picked our groups and drew lots. In the end, however, the first group to jump wasn't drawn by lottery. We decided that since the British fellow had a contact close to where we were, he should go first and try to contact the Resistance. He chose two other British soldiers and a British naval officer to go with him. Carefully, they removed the wood, stuck a hand through the hole in the door, and released the wire. As predicted, the door swung open. It was night, and I caught a glimpse of starry sky. We strained to watch as they jumped from the moving train and rolled to the side of the grassy hill. The door swung shut, then banged back and forth. "Where's the wire?" someone asked. No one knew. It must have fallen to the ground when they removed it.

"No matter," we decided. "Who's next?" A group of four went next, then another group of three. I had drawn Lot 5 and would be up soon, jumping with Norman and the two lieutenants I had been traveling with. As I prepared to jump, I reflected on my good fortune. Once again, I was going to escape.

Suddenly, there was a roar overhead; a deafening explosion rocked the train, and the open door swung wildly back and forth as the train shuddered to a halt. "What was that?" I asked.

"Looks like one of those British night fighters made a hit," one of the guys answered. "I don't think this train is going anywhere too soon."

Another explosion cracked the car open. Right in front of me, one of the prisoners was knocked backwards and I saw with horror that the top of his head was blown off. He didn't seem to notice; he was still talking. One of the guys in the car was a Jewish doctor and he rushed to help. Someone donated an undershirt to wrap his head, and I held him while the others went to help another injured prisoner. Looking down at him, I felt so bad. He was so calm; he didn't have any clue how badly he was hurt.

We could hear shouts in German as the guards swarmed around to find out what had happened. Quietly, someone pulled the door shut and held it as tightly as possible so it wouldn't swing open again. We replaced the wood in the hole and spent the night cooped up in that boxcar going nowhere and wondering what would happen next. Sometime during the night, the prisoner in my arms died.

The next morning we heard shouts in German outside the door. A series of thuds followed as someone swung something heavy against the side of the car. They had discovered the missing wire. A shout followed and the door swung open. Several German officers stood there, anger plain on their red faces. They saw the dead prisoner and yanked him roughly away from me and took him away somewhere. "Count them," the officer in charge commanded. Two soldiers entered the car, guns up, and motioned us to stand. There were 38 prisoners in our car—12 less than when we started.

God, they were mad. "Vere are they?" they demanded. "How did they get out? Ven? Vere did they jump?" None of us spoke a word.

"Someone will pay for this," they promised, and grabbed four guys at random, pushing them out the door. My friend Norman was one of the four. Colonel Good was another.

My heart was in my mouth as we watched the soldiers line the four of them up against the wall of a nearby barn and point guns at their heads. "Tell us or we'll shoot," they threatened. As I watched in horror, all I could think of was Norman saying, "I'll eat the bread now; I may not last three days." I guess he was right, I thought sadly.

But in the end, the soldiers didn't shoot. Instead, they got a pack of bloodhounds and wandered up the tracks looking for a scent, but as far as I know, they never found any of the escaped prisoners. The four soldiers who were singled out were thrown roughly back into the boxcar, and the Germans boarded it all up from the outside and nailed the door shut. Finally, they cut a two-foot hole in the end of every boxcar on the train. Right behind ours was the German troop car. Now the guards could look right into the cars and watch us at all times. They mounted a machine gun in the hole between their car and ours. "If anyone stands up while the train is moving, we'll shoot," they promised. Somehow, I had the feeling they meant it.

The next three weeks were torture. For 23 days we were in that boxcar, unable to stand or move around. In order to go to the bathroom, we had to crawl over to the waste drum and then lean over so the guards wouldn't think we were standing up. And the odor! You can't imagine how bad that waste drum smelled. The Germans only emptied it every couple of days, and sometimes it slopped over onto the floor. The heat and stench rose every day.

The first night one of the more resourceful soldiers fashioned a hammock out of a blanket he had. But he fell out and landed on another guy. That was the end of that. After that, everybody slept on the floor. We all lay down facing the same direction. Side by side, bodies touching, we could just fit. Partway through the night, someone would yell, "About face," and we would all turn over at the same time. It was the only way we could lie down to rest.

All we were given to eat was bread and water, and precious little of that. We were filthy, though we tried to wash with the little cup of water we were given. I wanted to brush my teeth in the worst way. A couple of the paratroopers had shaving equipment and we managed to shave once or twice. One fellow had deodorant, but he wouldn't let anyone use it. Even talking was subdued and without much substance because the guards stood right behind us looking in. Still, Norman Patrick and I managed to converse and became fast friends. We had both been raised in strict, Catholic families, and we talked about family, religion, and God. Norman Patrick had two rosaries that he had carried with him throughout the war. Now he gave one of them to me. "Seems like we can use all the help we can get," was his comment. I agreed.

Despite the awful circumstances, the soldiers tried to maintain some sense of normalcy. There was a small group of soldiers who had a deck of cards and played bridge every day. That was a game I didn't know, but I watched and learned from watching. One of the guys scratched the days off on one of the wooden slats each morning, and slowly we watched them add up: 10, 14, 18. I figured it must be nearly the end of July. Whenever the train slowed at a station, we peered through the cracks to see the name of the town we were in. This way, we had some idea where we were.

About a week after we were incarcerated, the train pulled off onto a siding at Tours, south of Paris, and just sat there for three days. Peering outside, we could see three bridges, two railroad bridges and a highway bridge, only about three hundred yards away.

That afternoon, the Americans flew overhead and began to bomb those bridges, but without doing much damage. The next morning, the B-17s came over at about 2,200 feet, and they just let go. The sound was deafening, and every time one of those bombs hit, the train would jump up and down on the tracks. We watched as they leveled one of the railroad bridges, terrified that the train would be hit again. Later, the Americans returned and took out the highway bridge. Smoke and fire rose from the rubble. I didn't see how we could ever survive this attack, but somehow we did, and one of the railroad bridges remained standing too. We stayed in that rail yard for three days under constant strafing from the Americans, sure that every hour would be our last.

Finally, the train moved again; I suppose they had been repairing the tracks and making a new plan. Now we took a

B-17 bombers strafe enemy targets

Clark Special Collections Branch, United States Air Force Academy,
McDermott Library, and The Friends of the Air Force Academy Library

course north, then east of Paris, finally arriving at Reims, France, on the 23rd day.

At last they let us out of the boxcar. After being cooped up like that for so long, many of the guys couldn't walk. They fell when they were pulled from the train and stumbled, crawled, or were dragged to the camp. There, we at last had a hot meal: some watery soup, a slice of bread, and some kind of mint tea. Even though it was so little, it was such a welcome relief to be out of that stinky boxcar, to see light, to walk around, even a little bit. We all looked terrible; our clothes were wrinkled and filthy, we were pale from lack of sunlight, weak from lack of exercise, and everyone had lost a lot of weight. If our parents or sweethearts could have seen us then, they wouldn't have recognized us as the handsome, fit youths they had sent off to war.

The French Resistance

France was occupied by the Germans beginning in 1940. From the beginning, the French attitude toward the German occupation was complicated. Most French citizens went along with the Germans because they wanted no trouble and feared the consequences of resisting German authority. Some of the French actively supported the Occupation because they felt the German authority was better than Communism, which seemed to be the alternative. Still other French citizens actively participated in underground Resistance activities, spying and relaying information to the Allies, blowing up German communication and transportation lines, and even providing an underground army that could slow the movement of German forces.

The French Resistance had grown from 1940 into a considerable force by early 1944, when the Allies launched D-Day. The Resistance had many weaknesses, including poor communication, a lack of adequate arms, and little support from the general population. However, the Resistance had many assets, too, including incredible bravery and willingness to make personal sacrifices.

Most of all, it was behind enemy lines, and the information its people were able to provide to the Allies was reliable and invaluable. They could also sabotage railroad lines, bridges, and centers of communication, and generally kept the Germans confused and busy putting out fires.

We only stayed in that camp for two days, then we were herded back into the boxcars, and the train moved once more. As we headed east, we knew the worst: they were taking us to Germany.

Then, close to Alsace-Lorraine, just before the border leading from France to Germany, an incident happened that gave us hope. Suddenly, the train screeched to a halt, and, peering out, we could see the berets of French Resistance fighters surrounding the train, shooting at the front and rear cars, where the Germans were riding. For the next hour and a half, a fierce shootout took place, bullets flying everywhere. Ducking our heads, we hoped we wouldn't get hit, and we prayed that we might be rescued. If the French could overpower the German guards, we would all be freed. Unfortunately, in the end, the

Germans proved stronger, and leaving four dead guards lying beside the tracks, they started the train and moved on. Dispirited, I watched the station get smaller and smaller along with my hope of ever being rescued.

This authentic 15-ton freight car of the "Karlsruhe" model is one of several types of boxcars used by Germans to transport prisoners. Its cramped interior would have held 80–100 people.

Courtesy of the United States Holocaust Memorial Museum.
Photograph by Arnold Kramer

Chapter Ten

Stalag Luft III

Two days later we arrived in Trier, Germany, where a big prison camp was set up. There, for the first time, we were registered with the Red Cross as official prisoners of war and given POW numbers. When I received my number, I realized that up to now, no one had had any idea where I was or what had happened to me. If I had died, no one would have known, and I would have been simply listed as missing in action. So it was with a bitter irony that I accepted my number. I had not escaped, but being officially captured had some small benefits. Being given this number constituted a kind of recognition—I had an "address" of sorts; my family would be notified that I was alive and could perhaps even write letters to me.

Colonel Good noted the day with an irony of his own. He was officially captured on the 30th anniversary of the day he had joined the army. His POW number was 50000. Mine was 50005.

We stayed in Trier for two days and then were moved again, this time by passenger train to Koblenz. The prison camp there was way up on top of a hill with at least one thousand steps up to the building where we were interrogated. Afterward, they marched us

> ### Kriegies
> When American soldiers were captured by the Germans, they became official prisoners of war, nicknamed "kriegies," from the German term for prisoner of war, *kriegsgefangenen*. Prisoners adopted the name kriegie with pride, and looked for ways to continue fighting the war through survival and elaborate escape attempts.

70

Stanley Edwards' POW identification card, with his POW number, 50005, on the back. Stan carried these tags in his pocket for nearly 60 years.

Author collection

into town. The Americans were bombing Koblenz, and there was a lot of noise and chaotic movement. While we were there, Americans leveled the water supply and the railroads in the town. We kept watch for them, and every day, just like clockwork, the 17s or 24s would come over, do their job, and go home. We cheered every bomb that fell. Some of us talked of trying to escape, but we were in Germany. Who would help us now?

In the end I stayed with the prisoners in this camp for about a week. At that time, five of us, all air corps, were told we were going to be moved. Norman Patrick Murphy was one of the five, but I had to say good-bye to the paratroopers that I'd traveled with all this long way. They were infantry and would be taken somewhere else. The five of us air corps pilots were put on a train and moved deeper into Germany. I remember seeing station signs at Dresden and Weimar before we finally stopped in Sagan, where there was a huge prison camp called Stalag Luft III. About ten thousand prisoners were held in this camp, which consisted of five compounds: north, south, east, west, and central. Each compound held a series of wooden barracks huts surrounded by seven-foot barbed wire fences. Guarding the perimeter were sentry towers, each built 15 feet above the ground and mounted with searchlights and submachine guns. It was a sobering sight.

Stalag Luft III prison camp

Clark Special Collections Branch, United States Air Force Academy, McDermott Library, and The Friends of the Air Force Academy Library

When we first arrived, we were put into solitary isolation cells for about a day and a half. These cells were tiny rooms with only a cot and a toilet, and prisoners were not allowed to talk to anyone or to have any personal effects whatsoever. There I felt the enormity of being a prisoner in an enemy country: alone, abandoned, and afraid.

Eventually, however, I was removed from my cell and placed in the South Compound, which housed only American prisoners. Norman Patrick Murphy was sent to the East Compound, with other prisoners from Canada and New Zealand.

At South Compound, I was interrogated once more, this time by an American lieutenant colonel they called "Big X." The point of his questions was to make sure I was really American, not spying for the Germans.*

Red Cross then gave me a new pair of shoes and a few items of clothing and I was shown my new home, a four-man room with two bunk beds in the corner. There were three men already in the room: George Sperry, a first lieutenant whom I quickly recognized as the group's leader, William Billig, a pilot who'd been shot down in 1942, and a quiet guy named Frank Saunders, who mostly kept to himself.

I arrived in this camp on August 27, 1944, and stayed there until January 26, five long months. After awhile, the days melted into routine. Every morning there was roll call on the grounds, and if that went well, we were given an aluminum pitcher filled with hot water so we could make instant coffee. If we had saved some bread from the

The International Red Cross

The International Red Cross is a humanitarian organization that registered prisoners and provided them with food, clothing, and medicines. They shipped food parcels monthly to all Allied POW camps except the Russians. Because food in Germany was so scarce during the later war years, many prisoners would have died of starvation and malnutrition without this service. A typical Red Cross parcel included sugar, concentrated soup, instant coffee, tins of biscuits, canned meat, orange concentrate, instant chocolate, prunes, raisins, powdered milk, powdered eggs, and processed cheese.

Contents of a Red Cross parcel

Clark Special Collections Branch, United States Air Force Academy, McDermott Library, and The Friends of the Air Force Academy Library

---

* These interrogations eventually formed the basis for the stories in *Beyond the Wire of Stalag Luft III*, a book that came out after the war containing short biographies of each man who was held prisoner there, and detailing how he came to be captured.

day before, that served as breakfast; if not, we just had coffee. Three times a week, they brought us "soup" for lunch. They called it soup, but it looked like what they did was cut the grass, boil it in water, and add some tallow to give it that greasy look. Still, it was hot, and that was a bonus. We also got half a Red Cross carton of supplies each week. These cartons always contained cigarettes, which we used to bribe our German guards into obtaining some fresh food: eggs, cheese, milk or bread. Sperry was the one who did the trading—we called him our "Black Market Officer." We became pretty creative cooks, combining things in new ways to make them seem more like meals. We even constructed a stove made out of a coffee can using little sticks and branches for fuel. It had a little crank on its side to keep the fire going. Each day, when we got our bread ration of one-third loaf, we would cut the crust off and save it. At the end of the week, we would combine it with raisins, dry milk, and a D-bar to make "godoyne," which was a sort of bread pudding. We'd put it on the window to cool, and sometimes it would get stolen, but that was life in the camp.

Kriegies cooking at Stalag Luft III

Clark Special Collections Branch, United States Air Force Academy, McDermott Library, and The Friends of the Air Force Academy Library

In the afternoons, I read a lot of books from the prison library, we played bridge two to five hours every day, and we were allowed to walk around the compound and see prisoners from other rooms. Officers conducted games and athletic events on the grounds to keep prisoners occupied. There were at least three radios in the compound (at one point I heard there were five). These were strictly forbidden, of course, so they were moved every few hours to a new location. In this way, we were able to track the progress of the war. Listening to the BBC gave us hope because we knew that the Allies were doing well and liberation seemed just around the corner.

I wrote letters to my family and neighbors, and of course, to Shirley. They were filled with the most trivial news because everything had to be read by a censor, but they kept me occupied. I kept hoping to receive a letter in return, but that day never came.

Reading this account of simple domesticity, you may think that we'd completely given up all thoughts of escape, but in fact, escape activities were going on all the time. There was an escape committee called X Committee that had been operating at Stalag Luft III for years. Almost from the beginning, I heard stories of their escapades, including the notorious tunnel break from North Compound. This break had occurred in March of 1944, five months before I arrived. The prisoners in North Compound had spent months laboriously digging three ingenious tunnels under the compound, which they named Tom, Dick, and Harry. Tons of sand had been removed and discreetly dispersed throughout the camp, and the tunnels shored up with bed slats. Forgers had prepared false documents, and tailors sewed and altered escape clothes. Guards were befriended and bribed into assisting and provided sample documents as well as helpful tools. Once involved, these guards remained silent for fear of reprisals from their officers. On the night of March 28, 1944, after months of work and narrow escapes, Harry had finally been put into service. Eighty-one men climbed out of the tunnel and hit the woods before a guard became suspicious and their cover was blown. Because this was the biggest prison break of the war, the alert went out throughout Germany, and all but three of the escapees were captured. Fifteen of them were returned to Stalag Luft III, but 50 men were shot and the rest sent to a concentration camp. By now this story was legendary in the compound. We knew what the risks of escape were, but prisoners felt that escape, or helping with escapes, was their duty. It was a point of honor among kriegies in the camp.

So the activities of X Committee continued, beginning with an interrogation of every new prisoner, such as I had faced, to be sure that they weren't spying for the Germans and also to learn what skills they had that might be used in escape efforts. Prisoners were reviewed for escape potential and the committee planned and executed escapes of those with the best chance of getting away. Because the Germans were using foreign nationals to work in the factories and war plants, it was relatively easy to pass as a foreign worker if you could speak a second language fluently. These were the men that were actively coached to escape. The rest of us helped with the effort. Billig and I both had good handwriting, so our job was to make out escape papers, forging documents to look like passports, visas, and work permits. We were given examples to copy and spent many hours painstakingly altering documents. We all made friends with the guards, figuring that a friendly guard might be amenable to taking a bribe. They were not strict; in fact, they tended to look the other way. We had trained the guards in our block to stop just inside the door and announce their presence, calling out, "Goon on the Block," after which all escape activity would stop until the guard left. Sometimes we'd invite one of them in for a cup of tea or a cigarette from a Red Cross package. Then we'd talk. I discovered that the guards didn't want to be there either. They were sick of the war, sick of service, and wanted to go home as much as we did.

One escape that took place while I was there concerned a prisoner named "Shorty" Spires. Shorty was a small guy who spoke five different dialects of German—in fact some people said he spoke German better than the Germans. What's more, there was a little guard who looked a lot like Shorty—same height and weight. Every night the guard would inspect the compound, coming in through the West door and leaving through the East door. Word was always sent ahead to the East side guards that he would be coming out.

So, tailors in the escape committee managed to make a uniform for Shorty that looked almost identical to the guard's. One night he put it on, and when the little guard entered through the West door, Shorty walked out through the East door. He marched confidently through the prison gates to the woods behind the compound, where he changed into workman's clothes. With his false identification, he bought a train ticket and went to Berlin, where contacts had been set up for him. When he met his contact, he was told to go south to Italy instead of north to the Baltic Sea, as there had been escapes there and the border was being watched closely. So Shorty climbed onto a train and headed for Munich, passing our prison camp on the way. At Munich, all passengers were stopped for questioning. While waiting in line for his turn, no doubt mentally rehearsing his story, Shorty felt a tap on his back. "Can you tell me what time it is?" someone asked in English. Shorty looked at his watch and answered—in English. The very ordinariness of the question had thrown him off guard. Unfortunately, the tapper was an SS officer. Shorty was taken into custody, brought back to Stalag Luft III and sent to solitary confinement, his escape activities momentarily over.

In this way, the time passed. We were always looking for ways to spice up our lives. We "celebrated" Thanksgiving, then

Christmas as best we could. In fact, for Christmas, we had decided that we would liven up the holiday by making whiskey.
For weeks, we had saved the little packets of sugar, prunes,
and raisins that came in the Red Cross packages, and now it
was time to put them to use. We put all that sugar and fruit
together with plenty of water and distilled it all through
somebody's trombone. The finished product was better than
we had expected. The resulting liquid was clear as a bell—
and about 180 proof! Everybody in the barracks was given a
glass. I sipped mine for about a week, but some of the others
drank it right down. Yes, indeed, that was some celebration.

We gave some of the whiskey to one of the guards, who
bolted it down. Next thing we knew, the guard was missing.
The alarm went out—the Germans were sure it was part of an
escape plot. They called us all together for roll call. Contrary
to the way things were usually done, they actually checked
picture ID's and compared each face against our picture. But
no one was missing. No one but the guard.

The next day he was found—quite by accident. After drinking the whiskey, he had evidently felt the call of nature and
gone to the outhouse. Being completely inebriated, he fell in
and disappeared. He must have fallen asleep at the bottom of it.
But once hauled up, he suffered no more than complete humilia-
tion, and probably quite a dressing-down from his superiors.

New Year's Day came, and 1945 was ushered in. The
weather turned bitter cold and the ground outside was frozen
and snow-covered. Escape activities were at a low point, and
prisoners turned to other diversions. In South compound was
a theater building that prisoners had built a couple of years
before, and we staged plays and comedy routines to pass the
time. The audience sat on chairs made from plywood crates
and always whooped it up and enjoyed the shows, many of
which featured the men dressed up as women.

On the night of January 27th, we were up at the theater watching a play when suddenly all activity stopped. Col. Charles Goodrich, the senior officer in charge, appeared on stage and made an announcement. "This camp is being evacuated. Russian forces are within 25 miles and all prisoners will be moved. The Goons have given us thirty minutes to be at the front gate. Get your stuff together and line up!" The audience buzzed with speculation. Where were they taking us? There wasn't any mass transportation. They must be planning a march. In this weather, that would be cold and miserable. If the Russians were that close, might we be liberated? Could we escape? Whatever would happen, we had just half an hour to prepare.

We hurried back to the barracks to gather warm clothes and provisions. I put on as many layers as I could find: undershirt, heavy wool shirt and sweater, and my army jacket. Remembering how wet my socks got when we were on the loose in France, I tucked three extra pairs of socks under my undershirt next to my body to keep them warm. We made up packets of raisins and prunes and sugar cubes that we had hoarded for celebrations.

Then one of our officers entered the room carrying something under his shirt. "Here," he said urgently. "We've dismantled the radios. Each of you, take several parts and sew them into the lining of your coat. When we arrive at the next place, give them to Big X so we can put them back together."

Even as we took the parts and began sewing, we were full of questions. "What about escape? Is that possible?"

"You're welcome to try," he answered. "Without papers, your chances on the loose in Germany are poor, especially if you don't know a foreign language. What you'd have to do is work your way back to the Russians and see if they'll return you to the Americans. But they'll be marching too; don't forget. And if you're going to do that, don't take the radio. We'll want it where we're going." We decided to take our chances with the Germans. It seemed too close to the end of the war to risk being shot as we left prison camp.

By 11:00 P.M., everything was ready. Guards came to the door. *"Raus, raus,"* they shouted. "Everybody out!" Bundled against the cold, we headed out into the night to join the long column of prisoners being marched west, destination unknown.

Chapter Eleven

The Long March to Moosburg

The night was clear and stars glimmered overhead. But the weather was bitter cold; the temperature was near zero with a 15–20 mile-per hour wind. The guards were grim and irritable as they pushed us along at a brisk pace. While we walked, I didn't notice the cold too much, the exercise providing its own heat. And though there were several inches of snow on the ground, those of us at the middle and back of the column didn't really notice because it was all churned up and trampled by those ahead. We spoke little, preferring to save our strength for whatever was ahead.

They marched us for 50 minutes, then allowed a 10-minute rest. At the third stop, an older guard fell back in step with us. He looked to be in his 80s. "Can't walk," he panted. "Too old." He looked terrible, pale and exhausted, with sweat pouring from his forehead. He dragged his rifle like he didn't have the strength to carry it. "Here," I offered. "Let me carry that for you." Gratefully, he handed it over as the guards called out, "All right, effrybody. Now march. *Schnell!*" and we started up again.

As we walked, me carrying the rifle, the old guard stumbling along as best he could, I offered encouragement. "You're doing fine, you're going to be all right. Just one step at a time," things like that. After another 50 minutes, they allowed us to stop again. *"Zehn Minuten,"* they called out. "Ten minutes."

Some of the prisoners rebelled. "We need more," they complained. "Give us half an hour. We've been marching for hours!"

"March or we'll shoot," the guards barked.

Forced Marches

As the war neared an end, it became common for the Germans to move prisoners rather than risk their being liberated. Jews were forced to march from concentration camps in the hope that American forces would bomb them, and their deaths could then be blamed on the Americans instead of the Germans.

Allied prisoners were marched out of Stalag Luft III and other prison camps so they could be kept as hostages. When the prisoners of Stalag Luft III were given their "marching orders" on January 27, the temperature was near zero, with four inches of snow on the ground. They marched in these conditions for two days before finding shelter on the floor of a tile factory in Muskau, where they stayed for 30 hours. After that they marched another 15 miles to Spremberg, where they were jammed into boxcars normally used for livestock. It was a three-day journey under hellish conditions until they reached Stalag VIIA at Moosburg.

Map of Germany showing prison camps: Stalag Luft III at Sagan, Stalag VIIA at Moosburg, and Stalag XIIID at Nuremberg (Nürnberg)

Clark Special Collections Branch, United States Air Force Academy, McDermott Library, and The Friends of the Air Force Academy Library

"Go ahead and shoot us," I heard somebody answer. "Come on. I'd like to see you try."

I was momentarily nonplussed, afraid for the speaker if not for the column. But he was right. The guards didn't shoot, and in fact, they did give us a half-hour rest. The old German lay down on the cold ground beside me while I sat down to change my socks, carefully placing the cold wet ones against my chest to warm them up. For half an hour we rested there on the path, talking dispiritedly. Then the guards were shouting, the prisoners groaning, and we were getting to our feet again. I picked up the old guard's rifle and turned to say something to him. Then I realized that he hadn't gotten up. He was still lying there in the same position. I leaned over and shook him, then saw that his eyes were wide open, staring straight ahead. He was dead.

"Stop!" I shouted. "Guards, come here. He's dead." Other prisoners stopped to look and a tight knot formed around his body. Several guards hurried over. "He was sleeping and he just died," we explained.

But the guards turned away, uninterested in the body. "Where's his rifle?" they demanded. "Who took his rifle?"

"I did," I confessed. "I was carrying it for him."

"Give it back," they demanded. "Hand it over. NOW!"

Prisoners rest in the snow on the long march to Moosburg

Clark Special Collections Branch, United States Air Force Academy, McDermott Library, and The Friends of the Air Force Academy Library

"All right, fine," I muttered, annoyed that they seemed to care more about the rifle than their fallen comrade. "You can have the damn thing."

We marched through the night and into the next day, stopping briefly each hour, longer when there was some shelter, a barn or a line of trees that broke the wind. Every few hours I changed my socks. Eventually, we came to an abandoned tile factory and stopped there for the night. The officers warned everyone about removing their shoes. "We've been walking for a long time, and if you take your shoes off now, your feet will swell and you won't be able to get them back on," they said. So, much as I hated it, I left my shoes on while I slept. But not everybody listened, and some of the guys took their shoes off anyway. In the morning, when we were ready to leave, they were sorry. Many of them found that their feet *had* swollen. They were unable to put their shoes on and were forced to limp along in stocking feet until they could put them on again. Frostbite was the word of the day. I was really glad I listened that time!

Tents at Moosburg prison camp, Stalag Luft VIIA

We had marched 54 miles in 92 hours. The next day, they put us on a train and sent us to Stalag VIIA, a prison camp at

Moosburg, north of Munich. The train was once again a box-car used recently for livestock, and we were stuffed in like sardines in a can. It was a three-day ordeal; filthy and stinky with the odors of human waste. All of us were sick with hunger, fatigue, and fear. It seemed too cruel to pull us out of the life we'd grown used to and throw us into these conditions again.

We arrived at Moosburg during the first week in February. I was told there were 127,000 prisoners from all different nations there. This camp was not nearly as well run as Stalag Luft III. The barracks were filthy, the sanitation was poor, and there was not enough room in the barracks for our men. Instead, 375 men slept in a huge tent out on the grounds. The tent had no floor. Prisoners were issued one blanket each and had to sleep on the ground.

When we arrived, our officers took command and tried to improve the situation somewhat. Colonel Good turned out to be one of those in charge. "Edwards," he asked me, "would you be willing to be a barracks monitor? We need to get these barracks cleaned up and the men acting like soldiers again."

"Of course," I replied, pleased that he asked.

The barracks I was to monitor was filled with enlisted men from all different outfits. I went up and introduced myself. "All right, men. I'm Lt. Stanley Edwards, and I've been told to get this place clean. You're going to have to take the straw mattresses off the bunks and hang them outside to air. I've got soap and water to wash all the bed frames, and then we'll wash the floor, too. We need to make this place shipshape!"

The men looked at me defiantly. "Tough," one of them said, and the others nodded. "We don't care who you are. We don't want to clean."

I looked at them, nonplussed. "Cleanliness is a real virtue," I said. "If you're not clean, you feel like nobody else is either. You'll have a lot more self-respect if you get this place cleaned up. You'll feel better about this whole experience."

"Not likely. Nothing is going to make us feel good about this." They grumbled and gave me lip, and I finally resorted to threats. "There'll be no food rations until this place is clean. Now get to work." It was largely an empty threat, but it seemed to work.

Eventually, mumbling, they pitched in, cleaning the place until it looked and smelled a whole lot better. The men felt better when it was done, too, and we got along fine after that.

I was in charge of that barracks for several weeks, and then they put someone else in there, and I moved out to the tent. Because I had developed a reputation for getting the Germans to give us fair food rations while I was in Stalag Luft III, I became the food officer for the tent. My tent mates had decided that instead of sleeping on the ground, we'd sleep together in teams of three. We spread one blanket on the ground, and three of us would lie on top of that with two blankets to cover us. It worked out pretty well. One night, though, a storm came up, and water just rolled through our tent, soaking everything. Some of us abandoned tent and blankets and fled through the rain to the nearest barracks, where we pounded on the door. "Please let us sleep here for the night," we begged. "Our tent is flooded." The guys in the barracks were New Zealanders and they were real nice. "Come in, come in," they responded, making room and even loaning us blankets. We spent the night on their floor, and in the morning, they pitched in and helped us clean up from the flood.

One of the guys that shared tent space with me was a fellow we called Slim. He and I became buddies and hung around together a lot. He helped me procure food from the Germans and worked with me on other tasks that Colonel Good assigned. It was nice to have a friend, but time at Moosburg dragged. There was very little food—often a loaf of bread had to feed 15 men—and the prisoners were sick and dispirited. Sanitation was a huge problem; the Germans never brought in the wagon to pump out sewage from the latrines and the toilets filled up. We'd fuss and complain; eventually they'd clean it up, but a couple days later they'd be full again. The Germans listened to their radios and reported that Germany was winning the war, battle after battle. But our officers privately listened to the BBC and told us otherwise. The Allies had crossed the Rhine, we heard. The German army was in a state of disarray. The war would be over soon. It gave us hope.

Then one day I heard that Shorty Spires was at it again. On March 1, Shorty and his buddy Vogel jumped over the fence into the enlisted men's compound and persuaded a couple of guys to exchange places with them. They went out on work duty as enlisted men, got them to create some kind of diversion, and then escaped. The rumor was that they were working their way through other prison camps using the same tactic. They'd switch places with a couple of soldiers, spend a night in their compound using their beds and food rations, and then be off. In this manner, they worked their way to the Swiss border, where the brother of one of our guards was hired to take them into Switzerland. I heard that the American Consulate paid him $20,000 apiece to take them across the border.

On the 15th of March, the Red Cross came into our camp bearing word that Spires and Vogel had indeed escaped. They had been taken from Bern, Switzerland, to England and then to the United States, where they were currently at Walter Reed Hospital in Washington, D.C. That was exciting—two of our own were back home.

But the Red Cross bore more ominous news as well. Hitler had given an order to shoot all POWs. There were some guns in camp, and our senior officers quietly got them ready, so we would have a chance if the order were to be carried out. But shooting 127,000 prisoners would not be an easy thing. The German guards realized that the war would be over soon and they began to dig slit trenches outside the compound to hide

Prisoners marking time in tents at Moosburg prison camp

Clark Special Collections Branch, United States Air Force Academy,
McDermott Library, and The Friends of the Air Force Academy Library

in when the bullets started to fly around the camp. Tension was ratcheted up another notch. Every day knots of soldiers gathered by the pump, gossiping and speculating. Something had to happen soon.

But a month passed and nothing much changed. Spring arrived, and the bitter weather modulated into gentler days. We spent more time out on the grounds, watching, wondering. Then one day, out of the blue, we were told that we could take a shower and walk outside the compound. We were all puzzled by that. We hadn't had a shower since the day we came to camp—all winter, we'd been washing under the icy cold pump. A shower sounded wonderful, but what did it mean? "You know," one of the guys whispered. "In Buchenwald, the Germans told the prisoners to take a shower, and then instead of spraying them with water, they turned the gas on them and killed them all."

"No," we answered in disbelief. "They wouldn't be doing that to people. You must have heard wrong."

"Seriously," the soldier answered. "I heard it from some-one who was there."

"Well, I'm not taking a shower," my buddy Slim stated flatly. "No way."

"I'll take a shower," I offered. "But only *after* I see guys go in *and* come out. Then I'll take my shower."

As it turned out, they did let us have showers, and the guys who went in came back out again. I took my shower, and it felt wonderful. Afterward, some of us wandered over to the fence. Some German girls were walking by. They knew a little English and stopped to talk. Suddenly, I felt young again, like the dirt and the war and the winter were melting away. It was just a spring afternoon in the country. Then a rough voice broke in. "*Nein!* You can't be talking to these girls. *Raus, raus!*" The guard sent the girls hurrying off down the road, and I was back to reality.

The next thing I knew, I heard a shell explode. I looked up the road to the north and saw five Sherman tanks on the top of the hill. They fired a shell, which hit just outside the camp, and another one that hit the administration building inside the camp. Chaos broke out. "It's the Americans," some of the prisoners shouted. "We're being liberated." Meanwhile, the guards were pushing us, trying to herd us back into the compound. An argument broke out as some of the SS officers ordered the Luftwaffe guards to go outside the fence to defend the compound. The guards refused, and the SS shot some of them on the spot. I couldn't believe what I was seeing. The Germans shot their own men! Other guards did leave the camp and went out to the slit trenches to man the defense.

The chaos inside the camp was unbelievable. Guys were pushing at each other like teenagers and shouting, "We're go-ing to be free!" Some of them climbed up to the roofs of the buildings to watch, but I thought that was foolish. I had seen a shell hit the administration building just minutes ago. I grabbed Slim and yelled, "I'm not going to have a stray bullet hit me—not now." We headed for one of the slit trenches inside the compound and listened to the battle.

The fighting lasted about an hour. The tanks rolled on down the hill, firing into the trenches and killing the Germans crouching there. When the tanks rolled past the front gate, we knew we were liberated. Slim and I and the others crouching in the trench got out and joined the party. Guys shouted and yelled and hugged each other. The guards didn't even try to keep order—they just seemed to disappear. Later, I realized that many of them had been shot trying to defend the compound and others had probably run away, hoping to avoid capture.

And so, finally, after all those months in captivity, we were liberated on April 29, 1945, by Patton's Third Army. It was indeed a day for celebration!

Patton's Third Army liberates Moosburg prison camp

Clark Special Collections Branch, United States Air Force Academy, McDermott Library, and The Friends of the Air Force Academy Library

Chapter Twelve

Liberation

Liberation was a curious experience. We were free again, but nobody knew what to do with it. The war wasn't completely over yet, and there were no immediate plans to send us home. General Patton visited the camp, and thanked us for our service to our country. "You are free men once more," he said. "The war will be over soon, and all of you will be sent home." Then he acknowledged that we'd been deprived of food and comforts for a long time and announced that he would send in a popcorn machine and we could all have popcorn, just like the American young people back home.

"Popcorn," some of the men marveled. "Can you imagine popcorn here?"

Patton did send in a popcorn machine. But can you imagine the chaos that ensued? One popcorn machine for 127,000 guys? The lines stretched all over the camp. I didn't even bother. I didn't want popcorn that badly—what I wanted was to leave.

Now that we were liberated, we could go outside the camp and explore the town, though not many of us did, having no money or transportation. However, I heard that a couple of the Russian soldiers who were POWs in the camp went up to town and raped two German girls. The story was that when Patton heard about it, he took the two guys, stood them up against a barn and shot them. When Russian officers protested, he said, "I'm in charge here. No one will commit rape on my command."

One day Colonel Good approached me with another officer named Richardson, who was also a C-47 pilot. He gave each of us some money and a bicycle and asked us to go on a scouting mission. "We want you two to ride around to the west and the north and see if there's a field out there big enough to land a C-47. What we'd like to do is lay five-foot steel sections down to make a temporary landing field, then bring in C-47s to evacuate all the prisoners."

What a lark to be able to ride off on bicycles, just scouting around. It was a warm spring day and the countryside was blooming with purple flowers. This was a genuine taste of freedom! It was an odd feeling after being incarcerated for so long. Soon after we started out, we found a brewery and went inside. We bought a glass of beer to toast our freedom—16 percent they said it was. I drank only a third of my glass before I felt woozy and had to push it away. All those months of privation had taken a toll.

We rode around all day looking for a possible airfield. At one point, we saw half a dozen German infantrymen without their rifles, just walking home. "How can they get away with that?" we wondered. We had been told that all German soldiers would be imprisoned, but there they were, looking tired and defeated. I thought, just let them go home. Just let this war be over.

Richardson and I rode all day, but we didn't find a single spot that would work as an airfield. Before heading back for camp, we stopped for supper at an artillery camp they were just setting up. The camp would have 155 guns that could shoot 25 to 30 miles across the river. There we learned that the Germans had blown up two bridges, and we wouldn't be able to cross the river until Seabees came in and built pontoon bridges that would allow trucks and tanks to move across.

The men in the camp invited us to stay for dinner. We found we could eat very little. We'd been starving too long.

When we left, the artillery people gave us packets four feet long by four feet wide to take back with us. "This is bread," they explained. "They're individual loaves that can be pulled apart, like buns. Take it back to the camp and share it with your friends." So we balanced them on the handlebars of our bikes and headed back to camp.

Colonel Good met us when we got back, and we had to tell him the bad news. "There's no place around here big enough to land a C-47. Nothing at all."

"We'll have to think of something else then," he said, then asked, "What's in the package?"

"Bread," I answered. "American bread." I shouldn't have said it. The next thing we knew, dozens of men were storming the bikes, shoving and pushing each other like animals to tear off the wrappers and grab the bread. Richardson and I backed off and disappeared. As I looked back, I saw the bikes dismantled on the ground and the men still shouting and fighting for a shred of food. I felt sick. It was a sorry sight.

With the C-47 evacuation plan dead, the officers had to come up with something else. With the help of the 155 outfit that we had met, the bridges had been built and trucks could move again. So the officers decided they would have to take everybody on trucks up to Landshut Airfield north of Moosburg. Because of the limited number of trucks, this would take a long time. It was determined that they would put every barracks and tent into a lottery to decide the order of evacuation. Bad news. Out of 127,000 prisoners, our tent drew the very last number.

I was frustrated and not inclined to wait around. I turned to Slim. "You want to try to make it on our own?" I asked. "We could hitch a ride up to Nuremberg and see if we can get out from there."

Slim agreed and we left the camp the next day. On the road we flagged a truck and asked if it was going to Nuremberg.

It was, so we climbed on the back and hitched a ride. It took two and a half hours to get there.

But I was weak from hunger and imprisonment, and the adventure proved to be too much. By the time we reached our destination, I was sick and shaking with fever and chills. Slim took me to Patton's headquarters, which was in a big hotel there, and they checked me into the hospital wing on the second floor. I weighed 116 pounds, down from 165 when I entered the service. I don't know what kind of treatment they gave me, but I know I slept a lot.

In the meantime, Slim was treated well by people at headquarters. He was able to talk to a finance officer, who gave him $200 for each of us to help us get back to the United States. They also gave us each a change of clothes.

While I was hospitalized, Slim made friends with a Red Cross girl who had a jeep, and when I was released, she took us to the airfield near Nuremberg. There, we saw at least 50,000 other POWs waiting to get back home. Many of them were really in bad shape, weighing no more than eighty pounds. They were just skin and bones, the wilted flesh hanging off their arms. I looked good in comparison.

Unfortunately, all over the airport were signs announcing that no plane was to pick up a POW. "What do we do now?" we wondered, looking around.

It had been a long time since I had seen an airfield, and in spite of my disappointment, I found it fascinating as always. While I watched, a C-47 landed and the pilot got out. He looked vaguely familiar. I maneuvered into position to meet him as he came off the field. Incredibly, it was a fellow I'd graduated with from flying school in the Class of 1943. We chatted for a few minutes, and I learned that my company was no longer in Grantham but had been moved to somewhere in France. Finally I confessed. "Look, my buddy Slim and I have been prisoners for a long time and we're dying to get out of here. Any way you can help us out?"

"Sure," he answered. "I'm on my way out to England to pick up a senior officer. But I can take you as far as Paris. Just casually wander over to the plane and get in. I'll be along in a little while."

We got into the plane without incident, and he took us to an airfield near Paris that afternoon. On the way, we passed over Frankfurt, and I saw how devastated the city was from all the bombing. It looked like a tornado had passed through.

When we arrived at this airfield near Paris, we wandered around, wondering where to go. We saw a jeep come by with a star on the side, meaning it belonged to a general. A staff sergeant was driving, and we flagged him down and told him our plight. He was on his way into town to pick up the general and offered to take us to the train station. So we climbed aboard and rode through the gates and into town without incident. This was lucky because we had no real identification.

We arrived at the train station about 2:30 in the afternoon but were told there would not be a train until 8:00 that night. By this time, every delay seemed intolerable. We both just wanted to move. We saw a freight train coming up the tracks going real slow and heading north. "You want to jump on?" I asked Slim. "It's going the right direction. I'm sure it's heading for Paris."

Slim agreed and we jumped into an open car filled with scrap metal. The train chugged slowly up the tracks, its engine throwing smoke and coal dust back at us. As we neared Paris, we saw fireworks. "I wonder what's going on," Slim mused.

We realized we'd better jump off the train before we hit the rail yard. We didn't want to risk a lot of questions. "When we see a road with traffic on it, let's jump off and hitch a ride," I suggested.

The plan worked, and we were able to snag a ride with a truck going to Paris. "What's going on?" we asked. "What's with all the fireworks?'

"We're celebrating," the driver replied. "Tomorrow has been named VE Day—Victory in Europe."

"Hallelujah," we replied fervently. The driver took us to Seine Headquarters. This was a big hotel in Paris that served as Eisenhower's headquarters in Europe. When we told our story at the desk, however, the staff sergeant told us that the hotel was completely full. "We can put you up in another hotel, though," he offered. Then he gave us three tickets: one was for the cab ride to the other hotel, one to pay for the room, and the third for breakfast back at headquarters in the morning. "Take a shower while you're there," he suggested. "You two look awful."

We got to our hotel and were given keys to a room on the 10th floor. It looked so luxurious, with a real bathroom and beds. We couldn't wait to clean up and lie down for a while. But we couldn't figure out how to turn on the water taps to take a bath. We fiddled and fiddled with it and finally called the front desk. They sent a chambermaid up. She was jolly and friendly and teased us as she ran the bath water for us. "You'd better get cleaned up and go out on the town tonight. It's going to be a big celebration. V-E Day!" She raised her fingers in the V for Victory sign.

We laughed and told her we wouldn't be able to talk to anyone because we didn't know any French other than *"J'ai faim."*

She grinned and said playfully, "There's only one phrase you need to know."

"What's that?" we begged.

"Voulez-vous coucher avec moi?" she answered with a giggle.

When we pressed her, she told us that it meant "Will you sleep with me?" and the girl would answer, *"Combien francs?"* meaning "How much?"

So we had our baths, got dressed and went down into the streets of Paris. It seemed as if the whole world was there, laughing and hugging each other and flashing the V for Victory sign.

Fireworks lit up the sky and music curled from the open doors of the bistros. Slim and I felt the $200 burning holes in our pockets. We went into the PX and bought cigars and Hershey bars, but we couldn't begin to spend the money. We never used the chambermaid's phrase, but we stayed out until midnight just wandering the streets and soaking in the freedom. Then we went up to our hotel room and fell sound asleep on clean sheets.

The next morning we walked back to Seine HQ for breakfast. On our way, a Frenchman approached us and asked if we had any soap. As it happened, I had squirreled away 20 bars of Swan soap from the Red Cross packages and had carried it all the way from Moosburg in a German ski troop bag. Delighted, I dickered with him and ended up selling the soap for $5.00 a bar American money. That gave us an extra $100. I was very pleased with myself as I pocketed the money.

When we reached Seine HQ, we were told that we'd have to be deloused before we could enter the dining room. They took our officer's clothes, gave us a really hot shower and a delousing treatment, then handed us a fresh suit of enlisted men's clothes and sent us to the dining room for breakfast. Even though the fresh clothes felt wonderful, I was sad to see my officer's uniform and warm jacket disappear. I would have liked to take them home for a souvenir of all we'd been through together.

While we were eating, a pilot that I knew came in. He'd been in my squadron at Grantham. I almost knocked my chair over trying to get to him. "Carl," I called. "Stan Edwards. Remember me?"

"Good God, Stan. Where in hell have you been?"

"Got a minute?" I asked. He sat at the table with us, and I told him the whole story.

When I finished, he just shook his head. "Wow. What a war," he marveled. "You want to go back to the squadron?"

"You bet I do," I answered fervently.

So he took Slim and me with him up to Orly Field in Paris where the general he was flying agreed to take us to my old squadron, now stationed on the northern coast of France. When we got there, I discovered there were many changes, of course. The squadron commander was new—our commander had been killed in a mid-air crash, but there were many guys I knew there. It was great to see them all again. "Well," the squadron commander asked, "would you like to go home with us?"

"You bet," I answered enthusiastically. "Can you take Slim, too?"

"We'll see what we can do," the commander answered. He took us out to Camp Lucky Strike, where he tried to obtain permission for us to go back with the squadron. But the answer was no. "You both have to go back with the prisoners," he told us. "But you're in the right place. Camp Lucky Strike is processing all the POWs in France for return to the U.S."

We said goodbye and wandered around Camp Lucky Strike trying to figure out what the procedure was. The first thing we did was look at all the tents and pick one out for ourselves. Then we looked for the quartermaster. We found his barracks, but no one was in there, so we issued ourselves blankets and all sorts of equipment, which we took to the tent.

We saw a lot of soldiers standing in a line and we asked someone what they were waiting for. "A milkshake," they answered. That sounded good, so we got in line. Then I noticed another line going a different direction. "Wait here," I said to Slim. "I'm going to see what that one is for."

I found out that they were issuing uniforms in that line— anything you needed: boots, shoes, field jackets, everything. So we left the milkshake line and got into the uniform line. We were issued brand-new officer's clothes from the inside out, including a new flight jacket. I was thrilled. What a terrific deal!

Later, we saw them setting up rows of tables. "I wonder what those are for?" Slim asked. So we hung around to see.

Soon, a truck drove up and dropped off another load of prisoners who went up to the tables to register. As we watched, we realized we knew some of the faces. "Hey," I shouted. "Those are the guys from our camp at Moosburg!" Sure enough, our tent mates were just arriving in camp. What irony! We had gone through all that adventure just to land in the same place at the same time we would have if we'd followed orders in the first place. We went up to the tables, shook hands and explained where we'd been. Then we joined them for registration, just as if we hadn't been AWOL for the last week.

We stayed there at Camp Lucky Strike for another two days. On the third day, they woke us up at 4:30 A.M., gave us a light breakfast, then moved us down to the port. There we boarded a big ship, the USS *LeJeune*, one of a convoy that was carrying some 4,500 prisoners of war back to the U.S. One of the officers told us that this ship had once been Hitler's yacht. It sank, was pulled out and refurbished by the United States, and would now carry us home. He gave me a picture of the ship, and I wrote the story on the back of it.

USS *LeJeune*, the ship in which Stanley Edwards returned to the U.S. Stan was given this picture by an officer on the ship. The story went that the ship had formerly been Hitler's yacht, which sank in South America. It was raised and renamed the USS *LeJeune*.

Author collection

By the time we finally got on board, it was about 3:00 P.M. and we were starving. So we flagged down an officer and complained, "We haven't had anything to eat since 4:30 this morning." The officer took pity on us and took us down to the Officer's Mess where coffee, doughnuts, and other snacks were sitting out on a table. "Help yourself," he offered. "But you'll have to do something for me in return."

"What's that?" asked Slim, his mouth already stuffed with doughnut.

"I want you guys to be responsible for one deck. Make sure the guys keep it clean and orderly. Can you do that for me?"

We agreed, and then came the best part. Because we were going to be in charge, they gave us a private stateroom, with just two beds and a private bath. It was like crossing on a luxury cruise! We did our job, and the trip back to the States was pleasant. From time to time on the way back, a fellow prisoner would ask us if he could take a shower in our stateroom. We always said yes.

We weren't allowed out on deck at night because submarines were in the area that might not know the war was over yet, and it could be dangerous. But other than that, there were few restrictions. Everybody had been issued $200 when they registered at Camp Lucky Strike (this meant that Slim and I now had $400 each), and there were card games all over the ship! There were some nurses on the floor above, and we'd go up there every afternoon and play bridge. But one afternoon a nurse and a soldier were caught having sex in the front gun turret. As a result, an order was issued saying that none of the men could go up on the nurses' deck. After that, we stuck to poker and blackjack on the lower deck.

The voyage to the States lasted 10 days. When we finally sighted land, everyone went on deck, cheering and shouting, jubilant to be home again. But the officers had determined that there were missing items: silverware and some really nice white navy blankets. "Nobody's getting off until all of the stolen items are returned," we were told. "Otherwise we'll have to search everybody's belongings." So the guys returned all the stolen items, and we finally docked at a port in New York.

When we stepped off that boat onto American soil, everyone, to a man, knelt down and kissed the ground. There were tears in my eyes as I stood up. I was so thankful to be back in the United States—so grateful to be alive.

Returning prisoners pass the Statue of Liberty

Clark Special Collections Branch, United States Air Force Academy, McDermott Library, and The Friends of the Air Force Academy Library

Chapter Thirteen

Return to Civilian Life

After landing, we were taken to Camp Kilmer in New Jersey where we gathered in a big auditorium. "All right, men," the officer in charge barked. "If you all pay attention, you'll soon be on a train to the post nearest your home. There you'll be given your 90-day leave." I was sent to Camp Briggs at El Paso, Texas, the base nearest to Phoenix, where my parents were living at the time.

We were all to board the same train, which was set up so the last car would be let off at each different city as we traveled west. The excitement on boarding the train was at a fever pitch. Everyone contacted the porter asking for whatever suited his fancy: beer, whiskey, food, snacks. I couldn't help reflecting on how different this train was from the one that had taken me to prison camp the year before.

Our first stop was Indianapolis, and everyone piled off the train with their $200 burning in their pockets trying to buy anything and everything they could get their hands on. One guy went on such a shopping spree that he missed the train when we pulled out. He went to the airfield and hitched a ride to St. Louis, which was our next stop. When we arrived, there he was, standing in the marshalling yard waiting for us!

The final stop was El Paso, Texas, where I was to get my leave. When we got there, we were told to figure out how much pay we had coming for the time we'd been prisoners. They said they would give us the back pay to the nearest thousand and mail the rest within a month. I had $4,340 coming, and to my satisfaction, they gave me $4,000 in one hundred dollar bills. I immediately went to the PX and got a money belt to secure my holdings. I was feeling mighty rich!

I flew from El Paso to Phoenix that night. Upon arrival, I didn't even call my folks at first. Instead, I went directly to a downtown bank and deposited the money for safekeeping. Then I called my parents. My mother told me that she'd first learned I was a POW in November and that she'd written me lots of letters, but they all came back. I asked her what she knew about Shirley.

"Oh my goodness," she replied. "You probably don't even know. Shirley joined the WAVES. She's stationed in Washington, D.C."

That night Mom cooked a huge dinner in celebration of my homecoming, but I could eat very little. My stomach was still too used to deprivation. That night, filled with excitement, I called Shirley. It turned out that she had been granted a two-week leave for her cousin's wedding in Chicago, which was to start on the upcoming weekend. I said I'd come to Chicago immediately. I couldn't wait to see her!

> **WAVES**
> The navy established the WAVES, **W**omen **A**ccepted for **V**olunteer **E**mergency **S**ervice, in August of 1942 to fill clerical positions at home as more naval men were needed at sea. Within a year, 27,000 women had volunteered. By the end of the war, women were performing a broad range of jobs in the aviation community, medical professions, communications, intelligence, and technology branches of the navy. When WWII ended, there were over 8,000 female officers and 80,000 enlisted WAVES.

"I'll meet you in front of Walgreen's Drug Store at the corner of State and Washington in downtown Chicago the day after tomorrow," I promised.

So I spent one day with my parents and headed back east to Chicago. I was burning to see Shirley but filled with anxiety wondering if everything would still be the same between

us. After all, there had been a
whole year and a lot of unusual
experiences since I'd seen her
last.

Stan's fiancée, Shirley,
in her WAVES uniform

Author collection

But when I saw her, standing in front of Walgreen's in her
trim navy blue WAVES uniform,
her beautiful hair cascading beneath the uniform cap, my
doubts dissolved. This was still
the girl I wanted to marry, and
luckily, she felt the same. The
only thing she didn't like was a
mustache I'd grown on the way
home. I promised to shave it off.
We talked about getting engaged, and then headed over to
Zobel's Jewelers where a relative of hers worked. We picked
out rings, and I put the engagement ring on her finger right
then and there.

We spent the two weeks of her leave in Chicago where
her cousin Oogie and her boyfriend Jim Feeney were getting
married. Shirley was standing up for them. That really put us
in the mood. We decided we wanted to get married right away.

When the two weeks were up, Shirley returned to Washington, D.C. I followed a day later. I wanted Shirley to stay in
the hotel with me, but she refused. "Not until we're married,"
she said. "Well, then," I countered, "we'll have to get married
today," and we took off to get a marriage license. Unfortunately,
we found out that in Washington, you had to wait three days.
That seemed like an eternity, so we drove up to Baltimore, got
our marriage license, and were married in the cathedral there
on July 3, 1945.

Upon returning to D.C., Shirley was told she could get a
leave equivalent to mine, now that we were married. We took

Stanley reunited with
his fiancée, Shirley

Author collection

off to Phoenix and spent the rest of our leave time with my folks, which was wonderful.

All too soon, though, the leave was up. Shirley had to return to Washington, and I had to go to Santa Barbara for more recuperation leave. I got the luck of the draw on that one. I spent every day playing golf and every night going to Hollywood.

After a couple of weeks, a fellow told me they were sending people to Santa Anna to be discharged. After all I'd been through, I had no more desire to be in the service. I just wanted a normal life. I applied for discharge immediately and was one of the first 27 to go to Santa Anna. When I arrived, I met several people who had gone through pilot training with me, and we had a great reunion. On September 15, I was officially separated from the service. I spent one day in Phoenix with my folks, but all I could think about was getting back to be with Shirley.

I hitched a ride on an airplane going to New Orleans, then another to Atlanta and another to Washington, D.C. Shirley and I rented a room with a bath for one month, but every day she had to go in to WAVE Quarters D. She wanted to be out of the service, too. At night she would come home crying, saying they teased her and told her she'd never get out.

I couldn't bear seeing Shirley cry, so I decided to take matters into my own hands. I talked to a sailor who had more stripes on his arm than a zebra. "Go see the head WAVE," he suggested. "I'll bet you can get Shirley out."

So I did just that. The head WAVE listened sympatheti-
cally but said there was nothing she could do. "You might try
Admiral ———," she suggested, and told me where he was
located.

I went to see the admiral. His secretary ushered me into
his plush office and told me that I could open the left side-
board of his polished mahogany desk and help myself to re-
freshments. The admiral showed up about fifteen minutes later.
"What can I do for you, son?" he asked, sitting ramrod straight
at the big desk.

I told him all about getting shot down, escaping from the
Germans four times, and finally ending up in prison camp. I
told him that Shirley and I had been separated long enough
and that she was longing to get out of the service so we could
have a real marriage.

He listened attentively to all of it, then asked, "Where is
she stationed?"

"WAVE Quarters D," I answered, and he immediately told
his secretary to get them on the phone. She did, and he spoke
into the mouthpiece. "Do you have a WAVE there by the name
of Shirley Edwards? Well, it's 2:00 P.M. right now. I want her
out of the service by 2:00 P.M. tomorrow. Do you understand?"

I sat there amazed that something like this was really
happening—but it was. I thanked him from the bottom of my
heart. "Now, if anything goes wrong, you call me at this number," he said. "It goes to my red phone for emergency use only.
I'll take care of it," he promised.

Lightheaded with my good fortune, I hurried back to
WAVE Quarters D, where Shirley was getting off her shift.
She came running out, excitement written all over her face.
"You'll never believe what just happened!' she cried breath-
lessly. "I'm being discharged."

I laughed and hugged her and told her what I had done.

"All I have to do is get a physical," she said, "and then
pick up my discharge. I can do it tomorrow."

We went out and bought railroad tickets back to Chicago for 3:00 P.M. the following day. We couldn't wait to get out of Washington, D.C.

The next day all went according to plan until the person who was to sign her discharge papers could not be found. We waited and waited, anxiously watching the minutes tick by. By 1:00, I was getting pretty nervous. Should I do it? Should I call the admiral on his red emergency phone? I decided to chance it.

He picked up immediately and asked to speak to the person in charge. "I'm giving them 15 minutes before heads start to roll," he promised.

Five minutes later, the discharge officer was in the room. He looked at us coldly, but signed the papers without speaking, and Shirley and I were off to civilian life.

Chapter Fourteen

Reflections

I'm 80 years old now, and when I think about that time, I sometimes wonder what it all meant. Four times I escaped from the Nazis and each time I was recaptured. I was in the war, and yes, I killed some of the enemy. But I was no hero. I didn't do much. For most of the war, I was a prisoner. Why did I survive when so many others died? And what did I learn from these experiences?

Stanley Edwards, 2002
Author collection

Well, I learned that you don't need much to survive. And when you're without food, not much else matters. All you can think about is where the next bite will come from. You're not picky. You don't care how food is cooked, or how it looks, or what it tastes like. You just want to eat. The will to survive is very strong. You can live through the harshest of conditions: heat, cold, rain, starvation. You don't think much about it. You just do what you have to do to survive.

I also think that I survived because I was young. When you're 22 years old, you never imagine that you could die. You are literally fearless. You take risks that you'd never take in ordinary life because you believe that you are immortal. And by the time you figure out that you aren't immortal, you take risks because you have no choice. That ability to take risks has helped me in life. I'm not afraid to stand up for myself or to say what I believe. I know that if you are unwilling to risk, you are as good as dead.

I was also lucky. I was lucky to meet up with experienced paratroopers who were equipped and trained to fight on the ground. They taught me that you make an impact wherever you find yourself, and that you never give up. All of those guys were so creative, so calm and matter-of-fact in the face of danger. Their ingenuity is typical of the American soldier in WWII, and I believe that is a large part of the reason we were able to win the war.

Finally, I learned that it's a very good thing to have friends. I would not have survived by myself. It took all of us working together to make it both in the open and, later, in prison camp. Even though I lost track of most of those guys and don't even remember all of their names, I will never forget them. I am bound to them by the extraordinary circumstances in which we found ourselves. Those of us who were together in Stalag Luft III prison camp held a reunion every year for 50 years. During that time, we came to know each other in better times. We pieced our experiences together into a crazy quilt of memories and were amazed by the connections and coincidences that kept us alive and meeting each other. And all of us know what it means to be grateful just to live.

For years, I couldn't talk about my war experience. And when I finally did, there were parts I was ashamed to tell. It took years of talking about it before I could finally own up to some of the awful things that I saw and did. I think part of the reason for that was because my father-in-law was German, and I didn't want to hurt him. But eventually I learned that talking brings healing. And understanding. And gratitude for the little things.

I don't know why I survived. My life since the war has not been extraordinary. I married the girl of my dreams and we had four beautiful daughters. As a family, we've had our ups and downs, and we don't always get along, even now. My Shirley died six years ago from a cancer that she battled for a long time. Now that she is gone, I appreciate more than ever what we had. An ordinary life.

That's what I want to tell young people of today. Live while you can. Spend time with your loved ones. Love and appreciate them. Make every day count. It's not what you accomplish in this life that matters—it's how you live it. Just do what you have to do. One day at a time.

The End of the War

By April of 1945, the war in Europe was almost over. Hitler's troops were meeting defeat on all fronts, and Germany was almost collapsing. American troops were advancing toward Berlin from the west, and Soviet troops were advancing from the east. On April 25, the two forces met at Torgau, 60 miles south of Berlin.

In Berlin, Hitler hid in his underground bunker as Allied air raids shook the city. On April 30, 1945, Hitler committed suicide rather than accept defeat. On May 7, 1945, Germany surrendered to the Allies. On May 8, Allies everywhere celebrated V-E Day. Victory in Europe was finally achieved.

But the war wasn't yet over. Japan was still fighting fiercely, even as Allied bombers pounded their cities and factories and sank their ships. In late July, the Allied leaders met to discuss the situation, and decided to drop the new Atomic bomb on Japan. On August 6, 1945, the United States dropped this bomb on Hiroshima, Japan. The blast killed at least 70,000 people, and injured as many more. When Japan still did not surrender, a second atomic bomb was dropped on Nagasaki on August 9, instantly killing 40,000 residents. Finally, on August 14, 1945, the emperor of Japan surrendered, and V-J day was celebrated. After six long years, World War II was finally over.

In the end, World War II was the deadliest in human history. It is estimated that somewhere between 30 and 60 million people were killed in battle or behind the lines. The Nazis had murdered six million Jews and another six million Poles, Slavs, and Gypsies in their death camps. Cities were destroyed and millions were left homeless. The costs of war were staggering, and its effects were felt for decades afterward.

Bibliography

Ambrose, Stephen E. *D-Day: The Climactic Battle of WWII.* New York: Touchstone Books, 1994.

The American Experience. 19 July 2001. http://www.pbs.org.

B24 Second Generation Research. United States Air Force Academy. 30 July 2003. http://b24.net/pow.

Behind the Wire: Stalag Luft III South Compound. N.p.: Arnold A. Wright, 1993.

Davidson, James West, and Michael B. Stoff. *The American Nation.* Needham, Mass.: Prentice Hall, 1998.

Escape from the Nazis. Secaucus, N.J.: Castle Books, 1975.

Holstrom, Carl. *Kriegie Life.* N.p.: Carl Holstrom, 1946.

The Longest Mission. N.p.: Association of Former Prisoners of Stalag Luft III, 1995.

On War: Maps of World War II. 06 June 2000. http://www.onwar.com.

Pictorial History of the Second World War. 06 July 2001. http://www.indstate.edu.

"Railway Car." Washington, D.C.: United States Holocaust Memorial Museum, n.d.

World War II Era Waves. Department of the Navy Historical Center. 01 April 2004. http://history.navy.mil.

Index

First names are given where known.

113

MORE GREAT WORLD WAR II POW STORIES AVAILABLE FROM WHITE MANE

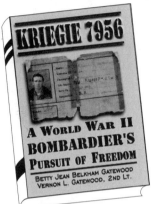

KRIEGIE 7956

One POW's Courage, Duty, and Dreams

The POW experiences of deprivation, lone-liness, and discomfort are interspersed with Vernon L. Gatewood's wit, humor, and in-trospection despite the desperate conditions in the three camps in which he was held for nine months after being shot down in his B-24 over enemy territory.

ISBN 1-57249-281-3 $7.95   (PB)

SHOOTDOWN

POW in Stalag Luft III after being shot down over Schweinfurt, Germany, in August 1943. Solitary confinement—relentless interroga-tion—a body-packed boxcar. Wheeler's real test of leadership was when the Germans evacuated 12,000 Allied POWs within the sound of the Russian guns.

ISBN 1-57249-310-0 $14.95   (PB)

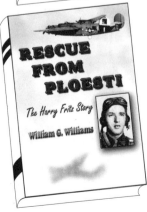

RESCUE FROM PLOESTI

B-24 tail gunner Harry Fritz experiences the threat of death several times during WWII in the skies over Romania, and as a pris-oner of war. As illness diminishes his will to live, he and 1,100 other Allied airmen are plucked to safety in a daring U.S. Army Air Force rescue mission.

ISBN 1-57249-340-2 $12.95   (PB)